HEALING
THE WHOLE
PERSON

HEALING THE WHOLE PERSON

A SOLUTION-FOCUSED
APPROACH TO USING EMPOWERING
LANGUAGE, EMOTIONS,
AND ACTIONS IN THERAPY

Robert B. McNeilly

Foreword by
Bill O'Hanlon

JOHN WILEY & SONS, INC.

New York • Chichester • Weinheim • Brisbane • Singapore • Toronto

ISBN: 0-471-38274-4

FOREWORD

I N RECENT YEARS, THERE HAVE been several exciting and radical developments in the areas of communication and change. The first is the rise of constructivism or social constructionism. This is the idea that reality isn't quite as fixed or set as we imagined it to be. Physicists tell us that reality shifts depending on how it is observed and measured and that there is no way to objectively measure reality because we are always changing it as we observe it. In the United States, there used to be a newscaster who was trusted by the nation who delivered the evening news. He ended every broadcast with his signature sign-off: "And that's the way it is, December 5, 1959." After many years, this venerable veteran finally passed the baton to a younger man, also trusted, but of a new generation. This new broadcaster had a new sign-off: "And that's a part of your world, December 5, 1999." How the world has changed since we were so certain that there was only one truth and we knew it. We "knew" that aborigines were "primitive" and that White, European culture was "advanced." We "knew" that women were less capable than men. Rob McNeilly shows how this development, more than being humbling and creating relativism, is an opening to many new possibilities.

Another development is in the area of language. Language has been found to influence our moods and emotions, our actions, and again, even our reality. When a superpower attacks and civilians are killed, it is called collateral damage. If it is your family, it is called murder or genocide. Abortion is called pro-choice or murder, depending on your view. The different words lead to vastly different feelings and actions regarding the same "reality." Again, Rob McNeilly shows how to use this new awareness of the power of words and the deliberate choosing of phrases and words to create an environment in which change naturally occurs.

In this book, McNeilly details shifts that may at first glance seem simple but are actually quite profound. He invites the reader to shift from a focus on problems to attending to concerns, which opens up entirely new ways to solve dilemmas. He also invites a shift from problems and pathology to an appreciation of resources, competence, and solutions. Last, he invites clinicians to move from an authoritarian, expert position to one of partnership and collaboration. All these shifts, while producing profound results clinically, can have the unexpected benefit of reducing stress and burnout for the clinician who adopts them.

Rob McNeilly has written a clear and practical guide to the latest developments in the counseling field. His concern with ethics and respect shines through the text. Filled with engaging anecdotes and an accessible style, it is sure to bring an all too uncommon common sense back into clinical work. Buy it, read it, and use it.

BILL O'HANLON

Santa Fe, New Mexico

PREFACE

I<small>N WRITING THIS BOOK, I AM</small> acutely aware of Lao Tzu's comment

> Those that know do not speak,
> Those that speak do not know

and also of the perception of brief therapy as cold and emotionless. I offer an additional perspective to counter those comments.

I have written about my personal experiences and examples from my practice with a background concern to emphasize what I have come to appreciate as a main theme of this work, namely to reconnect our work and our clients' experience to everyday life, reminding us of our humanity and our necessary limitations, and to invite acceptance of our perfect imperfections and avoid the agony of attempting the unattainable. I have attempted to keep theoretical explanations to a minimum, hoping that readers will make their own individual understandings, which will be more fitting and useful.

I am impressed with the elegant and simple power in this approach—the way clients can accept their experience, shift their focus, and get moving again. I am also impressed with the benefits I observe in practitioners learning this approach, in their effectiveness and personal and professional satisfaction.

I feel privileged to be a small link in the evolving chain of conversations designed to enhance our mutual sense of settlement, satisfaction, and ability to live together in a mutually respectful, mutually sustaining, mutually peaceful world.

ROBERT B. MCNEILLY

Melbourne, Australia

ACKNOWLEDGMENTS

I AM GRATEFUL TO MY FAMILY—parents, brother and sister, children, and especially my wife, Cherry, to whom I owe my life.

I am grateful to my teachers, preeminently Milton Erickson, and also Humberto Maturana, Julio Ollala, and Rafael Eccheveria, to name a few.

I am grateful to "Australian Doctor" for their support in initiating this project.

I am grateful to Lorna Seabrook for her meticulous proofreading and encouragement, and to Tracey Belmont from Wiley for her innovative and generous ideas and persistence.

R. M.

CONTENTS

INTRODUCTION

"IT IS MY EXPERIENCE THAT THERE isn't anything that can be achieved taking a short time that can't be achieved almost as well taking a much longer time." This paraphrases the words spoken by Dan Ackroyd's character as he received a standing ovation for his contribution to therapy in the film The Couch Trip. Ackroyd played the role of an escaped psychopathic criminal who stumbled into the position of locum for a Beverly Hills psychiatrist going to London to have his nervous breakdown in hiding. Ackroyd's character didn't know the rules of psychotherapy, so he cut right through them with amazing results, curing people by the busload.

People have always been fascinated by the miraculous and the spectacular, and in our present instant society, a lot of people are looking for a quick fix. It's not surprising that brief therapy is on the rise, with added impetus from the bottom-line mentality of managed care executives and economic rationalists and their concern for time and cost sensitivity.

Brief therapy has been criticized for being superficial and trivial, not plumbing the true depths of the real issues, skimming over the surface of problems, abbreviated, cold, even Gestapo therapy. It is actually an approach that fits our times precisely: fast moving, future oriented, action oriented, demanding instant answers. At the same time, variations are appearing—solution-oriented or solution-focused therapy or counseling—that are a more accurate reflection of the mood of the best of this approach.

Solution-oriented therapy tends to be less concerned with the explanations of causes than with future outcomes. Einstein's inquiry "Does the next station stop at this train?" puts explanations in their rightful place: after the event they were supposed to explain. This approach shifts the ground from thinking of the problem as a pointer to the "real" problem to considering that the problem *is* the problem. Avoiding the problem is no longer taken as a sign of avoiding "reality" but is recast in the role of a solution. A lot of time and suffering may be averted in the process.

In an increasingly complex and unknowable world, we find ourselves facing challenges no other generation has faced. Balancing on a moving carpet instead of looking for solid ground is an ever present concern. This shift in our paradigm includes an invitation to wonder, to not try to grasp meaning, to respect mystery rather than measurement alone, to value transparency rather than insight.

The structure of counseling, like so many other aspects of life today, is changing. Agency workers are becoming even more overloaded. Many counselors in private practice are concerned about diminishing numbers of clients even while there is a growing awareness that with the accelerating pace of life counseling is more and more important. It has been claimed that counseling is a major growth area. But how can an agency counselor fit it in? How can someone in private practice offer counseling to clients with a sense of being genuinely competent, given that for many of us, the counseling that was a part of our training seems no longer relevant to the plethora of situations that were rare or nonexistent then, such as anorexia, bulimia, ADD, ADHD, OCD, codependency, and so on? Until recently, the only options we seemed to have were to listen attentively and respectfully to our clients and, if more was needed, to refer clients to a long-term psychodynamic therapist or psychiatrist or get more training ourselves.

Fortunately, there is another option:

A woman in her early 40s consulted me for counseling because of recent difficulties at work. She sold insurance over the phone and was expert at it. She loved her work, and trained new telephone salespeople about how to deal with difficult customers, how to cope with rudeness and a recurrent "no." Her problem was with her new boss, who was demanding and unsupportive; nobody liked him. After we had talked for about five minutes, I said, "So your new boss is a difficult customer." Her jaw dropped, she was silent, lost in thought as the connections began to fall into place. "Thank you," she said. "I'll be OK now." And she was. There was no need to ask about any issues with authority, needing to be in control, resisting change—just a way of connecting her resources and her problem.

We know from our everyday experience that words and language can harm or heal, that emotions and language have mutual influence, and that emotions influence health.

A man called for an appointment, asking if counseling could help his headaches, which he had been suffering from daily for 12 years. He had been thoroughly and repeatedly investigated for organic causes, and all tests were normal. I suggested that it would be important that he brought the headache with him, so we would have something to work on, and when he arrived for his appointment, he was bemused by its absence.

When he said that he didn't have a headache, I asked him what he did have. When he stated that his head wasn't tight,

I asked him how it was. When he discovered that his head didn't feel pressured, I asked him how it did feel. After 10 minutes or so of this conversing to and fro—he stating how his experience wasn't, and I asking repeatedly what his experience was—he suddenly exclaimed, "My head's comfortable!" This was apparently the first time in the 12 years since he had been suffering from the headache that he had really noticed the comfort. Previously, it wasn't aching yet, it wasn't tight at the moment, but always, as a direct result of his use of language with himself, he was always on the verge of a headache, not noticing its absence as an experience but as just a temporary lull in the storm. He continued to be delighted to learn how to enjoy his comfortable head and to experience its increasing presence.

As with the woman with the difficult boss, we avoided a prolonged intake session and instead seized the opportunity to connect resources and problems to generate solutions.

We are also aware of the importance of emotions and the body in our everyday life. Our emotional experiences are triggered by events that change our experiences drastically and also influence what we can and cannot do, who we can and cannot interact with, which possibilities open and which close for us. We are also aware of the profound influence our body has on us: going for a walk in the park can shift our thinking so we can solve a difficult problem; the relaxation of sitting reading a book on a holiday refreshes us long after we return to work; the pleasure of a hot bath after a strenuous day in the garden can melt away the stresses of the day. But we have given insufficient attention to how we can make better use of our ability to observe and to directly influence our emotional state or our bodily experience.

The challenge for us is how to provide care, including counseling, to our clients so that we can offer effective help and at the same time fit in with the structure and time constraints of contemporary practice. How can we find a counseling method that is time efficient and results oriented?

The method this book describes is just that. Solution-oriented therapy can get to the core of the issue without needing to obtain long and detailed information about the past, childhood traumas, or deep understandings of transference and countertransference. There has been a change in our social values away from an archaeological digging up of the past toward designing future outcomes. Of course, sometimes taking a long and detailed history of the past will be necessary, but it isn't always, and to force such a process on someone who doesn't need it could be an unhelpful or even harmful intrusion.

The ideas in this book are derived from my own study and my learning from some world authorities in the field, such as Milton Erickson, Steve de Shazer, and Bill O'Hanlon, who have written books that explore more deeply the background of this approach. In each of the chapters I address a particular technique relevant to clinical practice and offer case examples and some questions to help you translate these ideas into your own style. My experience in teaching counseling to health professionals over the past 22 years convinces me that the skills that stick and are put to use are the ones we have related to our own particular manner and methods.

In short, solution-oriented therapy is another effective tool to choose when we work with clients. Older, more time-intensive methods such as psychoanalysis may sometimes be warranted but not always. In the film *Lovesick*, Dudley Moore plays an aberrant New York psychoanalyst whose work is supervised by Freud's ghost (Alec Guiness). Toward the end of the film, Freud's ghost appears in a straw hat, brightly colored shirt, shorts, and sandals and tells Moore, "I had some great ideas back then, but you all took them so seriously. I'm off to New Mexico to do some group dreaming!" I invite you to follow along, to try out the ideas behind solution-oriented therapy with yourself or your clients and see what you discover.

CHAPTER
ONE

General Principles

WE HUMANS ARE LINGUISTIC BEINGS, we are emotional beings, we are conversational beings, we are concerned beings, we are embodied beings.

LANGUAGE AS ACTION

Martin Heidegger, a contemporary philosopher, pointed out that experience is a breaking down of the transparency of everyday happenings. Our daily experience makes us value transparent, unaware activities such as walking and writing, even complex tasks such as driving a car and conversing with another. The complexities of such interactions don't allow for aware action and can only be achieved automatically.

A cornerstone of the solution orientation is an obsession with language. Both Heidegger and biologist Humberto Maturana have emphasized the action component of language in their work. Because most of us are doing talking therapy, this has to be a prime focus.

Following Milton Erickson's lead, Steve de Shazer and Bill O'Hanlon, as innovators in the field of contemporary psychotherapy, have written extensively about the use of particular language forms to facilitate change in clients. They use what are called presuppositional questions to stimulate new thought patterns in their clients. These at first strange-sounding questions are specifically designed to stimulate the search within the client's experience for some relevant resource, change, or direction in the client's life. Clients might be asked, "What could we talk about together today

3

so that some useful change could happen for you?" or "What changes have you already noticed before you even decided to make an appointment?" or "What's happening when the problem isn't there?" or "If a miracle happened and the problem suddenly disappeared, what would be different in your life and how would you notice it?" These questions can be delightfully refreshing. They invite active engagement by the client, a mood of expectancy for a desirable outcome, and help to generate a sense of normality and humanness. Just as delightful is the invitation at the end of a session for clients to pay attention to their experience between sessions, noting particularly what's happening when their life is going well and they are handling things the way they want to be handling them.

These conversational moves can have a profound impact on clients' moods and their progress toward generation of their own solutions. The therapist also benefits from the reflected glory—and from not getting exhausted, like the cursed Sisyphus pushing the same boulder up the same hill over and over again.

Likewise, language can also change the tone of therapy from one of hope to one of despair. I overheard my 14-year-old son's friend saying that a family friend had been given a "death sentence." When I asked him for details, he reported that the family friend had been to her doctor for information about her breast cancer and on asking "How long do I have to live?" was told "You've got six months." It wouldn't surprise me if the death sentence had been carried out early. I'm sure the doctor thought only about giving information and was probably totally unaware of the impact of his comment. What a difference it could have been to say "six months might be usual, but no one can say how much longer you might live."

EMOTIONS AND THERAPY

Are emotions mandatory? Are they a nuisance? Some therapists' offices have facial tissues conspicuously placed as an indirect imperative to emote. A reluctance to cry has been seen by some as avoiding the issue; in the 1960s we were encouraged to let it all hang out. Emotions were considered to be like fluids, subject to the principles of fluid dynamics: they must not be held down or held in or there might be an abreaction as a sudden and unwanted release of all these pent-up experiences. They must be expressed even if and perhaps only if they cause discomfort. Repression would cause pressure to build up, leading to stress unless release could be achieved. Some clients were encouraged to relax so the pressure would dissipate.

Who hasn't felt better after a good cry or a good shout at a football game? On the other hand, who hasn't had the experience of discovering that the longer the tears flow, the more there are to flow; the harder the cushion is thumped with the baseball bat, the more anger there is to expunge? Sometimes, expressing emotions is the *cause* of the emotions, not the experience of relief. Expression can be the solution and sometimes the problem.

Emotions have also served as signposts to hot spots in a client's psyche. When we notice the client's eyes are filling up or widening in fear or the client's knuckles are whitening from gripping the arm of the chair, we might ask, "Is there something that's upsetting you about that?" and take the response as an indication to go searching for some juicy information. Although all of these ideas about emotion can be useful in the process of clients finding their resources and solutions, there is another vantage point emerging.

LANGUAGE AND EMOTIONS

Just as emotions are the context within which language can occur, language can also influence the kinds of actions (i.e., emotions) we perform. Humberto Maturana, in several of his Australian workshops, spoke of the braiding of language and emotions as a conversation.

We are all familiar with clients who are frightened of going to the supermarket and are likely to avoid that experience, thus reinforcing their fear. Interacting linguistically with them may help to shift their emotion to one of possibility or even confidence so that they can then take new actions and reinforce the more desirable emotions of confidence and security. If we can generate a mood of trust in clients, they are more likely to be able to speak about issues and resolve them to their satisfaction. Also, if we can help them to resolve their concerns respectfully, they are then more likely to trust us. Trust generates results and results generate trust.

THE BODY AND EMOTIONS

By considering the *body* as a whole, we can move beyond mere observations of body posture, body movement, and body language and create another domain of observation, design, and interaction. By examining the *embodiment* of emotions and experiences, we can move beyond "reading" someone's body language by decoding some supposed universal language and generate the possibility of directly influencing the context or background of the problem. By shifting the ground of the problem, we may be able to transform it or dissolve it.

We can consider the body as the embodiment of language, emotions, conversations, experiences, and accumulated learnings. This is very closely aligned with Milton Erickson's notion of the unconscious as a vast storehouse of accumulated life experiences and wisdom on which to draw. We know from our everyday experiences that memories can trigger bodily reactions: The thought of food can prompt salivation and stomach rumblings (and the presence of a little wiggly thing can remove the desire to eat in an instant); the memory of an absent lover can lead to a change in blood circulation; the idea of meditating can generate the body sensations of preparing to meditate or even the meditation experience itself. We also know that much of our learning has become automatic, when our body responds without the need for our awareness; signing your name, putting the car keys in the ignition, dialing a familiar phone number, all of these and a large range of other actions are experienced as if they were a direct expression of a body process. It really is as if the body just does what it does.

Certain emotions are associated with certain body positions just as certain body positions are associated with certain emotions. Think again about Einstein's question "Does the next station stop at this train?" Many people experiencing anger find that they are gritting their teeth, but when a friend had his teeth wired together following a fractured lower jaw, he reported that he was very irritable. We could speculate that the irritability was not only related to the pain and awkwardness, but was also contributed to by the body position of clenched teeth. When I have invited people to intentionally clench their teeth, most report an emotion of some sort of anger.

By observing the body, we can make speculative interpretations about the emotions that individual may be experiencing. But we can also shift the body position to facilitate more desirable emotions that will then allow for the actions that constitute the solution the person wants. If a client talks about his fear of public speaking, we can anticipate that he is concerned about a future appearance and ask what it is that he is so concerned about. We could also invite the client to stand in a body position of confidence, with feet firmly on the ground a shoulder-width apart, shoulders back, and head erect as if looking into the distance. Changing the client's body position could facilitate an emotion of greater confidence, and the possibility of speaking publicly may no longer seem so remote. By practicing the body position, the actual speaking can be facilitated.

CHAPTER TWO

Language in Counseling

We ARE BEGINNING TO EMERGE FROM a 2,500-year tradition of thinking of language as purely descriptive: by naming an object, we assume we are describing it. In the philosophy of language, philosophers are beginning to look at language, not just through it. If we wear yellow glasses, we will see a lot of yellow; if we wear the glasses of a particular political party, what we see is influenced by those politics (the opponents look wrong). Language as we have used it has revealed a rich world of observations but has blinded us to our looking.

If we examine our everyday experiences, it becomes obvious that when we speak, we want an action to happen. When we say to our child "You're untidy" or "Your math grades aren't what they could be," we are saying this to produce tidiness or improved math grades. We have all heard examples of language resulting in future action so that we need to be careful in what we say. Our words can harm or heal.

This awareness provides us with a direct way of influencing our clients' experience. Obviously, we can't guarantee that saying "You will be okay" will make it so, but by saying "People have survived worse," we can at least create, in our client, the possibility of surviving. With careful and responsible use of language—what we say and don't say, how we say it, and how we appear as we say it—we can help our clients choose the best possible option.

PRINCIPLES OF THIS APPROACH

When we ask different questions, we get different responses. We all know that what we say is important, but how can we say something useful?

A couple arrived first thing Monday morning. I asked them what I could do to help. The wife stated that they had stopped communicating and were often fighting, to which the husband replied that no wonder they were always fighting when she nagged all the time. Within a few minutes there was the problem for all to see! My question had helped to precipitate it, and we all had to work hard to rescue the situation.

Asking a client, "How is your anxiety today?" leads the conversation in one direction; asking "What improvements in your mood have you noticed since the last visit?" leads it in another. "What's the problem?" is different from "What would you like to get some help with?" These differences are not merely semantic. They actually help to create a different experience and outcome for the client.

In the following chapters, we will look at how using a particular kind of question can move the counseling process along in the direction we want and, even more important, in the direction the client wants. We will ask questions that may sound a little strange at first, but most likely, our clients won't find them strange at all but will report satisfaction that they are getting relief.

Examples of these questions include "What changes have you made since you made the appointment? What is it like when the problem's not so bad or not there at all? What might you do to have more of the solution? How can you ensure that the improvements continue? How would you cope better now if the problem returned?"

In our training, we learned skills in problem orientation that are essential for effective clinical practice, but these skills don't necessarily translate into the delivery of counseling. In a counseling session, too much emphasis on pathology can even exacerbate the problem. It turns out that counseling conversations can benefit from an approach that focuses less on pathology and more directly on outcomes:

Another couple arrived a few days later, and I asked them what had happened since they had decided to make the appointment. The husband said that his wife had told him about the appointment, and when he asked her why she had made it, she told him she was worried about why they weren't getting along as well as they used to. He told me that after this, they sat down and had a long conversation about her worries, her concerns, her fears, his uncertainty, and his surprise, and as a result, things had begun to improve dramatically. I asked them what they had learned from their conversation, and they both recognized that they needed to spend more regular time talking with each other, sharing some activities, and they had already decided how to do that. They were going to have coffee down the street each Saturday morning; they were going to go to the movies together at least every two weeks. After about 10 minutes, we were all very pleased with the result, and yet what had happened? All I needed to do was to help them see what they had done that would be helpful, so they could do more of that, instead of delving into their unconscious mire (we all have such a place, and we could all get pretty messy if we were to delve there).

As noted earlier, solution-oriented therapy is not always the answer, and sometimes delving into the past will be not only helpful, but essential. However, sometimes, and perhaps even usually, such depth is not necessary to effect positive outcomes for our clients.

Generating the Therapeutic Relationship

I like to begin a counseling session, like any social conversation, by asking some general questions, such as "How's the family (the garden, the favorite football team, or whatever)?" If I don't know the person, I find it helpful to spend a few minutes asking about hobbies, leisure activities, and what the client does for fun. Asking these everyday kinds of questions helps to set a mood of normality and ordinariness, with counselor and client on a more even level. This normalizing stage can itself help the healing process:

A GP who is focusing on counseling in her practice wrote, "Asking about hobbies, leisure time, etc., usually shifts the emotion of the consultation, so the [client] becomes more confident, more animated, usually accompanied by smiles, a softening of facial features, and an opening up of body gestures. I find myself almost breathing a sigh of relief. The question takes the pressure off me in some way and increases my rapport with the client."

One of the characteristics of a problem is clients' fear and certainty that their experience is unique, horrendous, and extraordinary, and that they are uniquely, horrendously, and extraordinarily defective. These characteristics make the problem so much harder to even begin to address because clients feel overwhelmed. By changing the client's mood from feeling overwhelmed to feeling more capable, the problem can be experienced as more manageable. Sometimes this change even leads to a comment such as "Now I know where to begin, I'll be okay."

If a client comes in distressed, frantic, or in pain, it would obviously be disrespectful to ask these questions. They would seem trivial and might damage the trust in the counselor and so are best avoided. But in most situations, such lead-in conversations are very useful, and taking a few extra minutes at the beginning of the consultation can often save many minutes, and perhaps even hours or weeks, as the counseling process unfolds.

Milton Erickson once told me that he thought clients had enough on their hands coping with their grim problems without having to put up with grim treatment as well. He asked me, "Why don't people have more fun in life?" He told me that once when he was a younger man, he was walking to his seat in a small plane, and when the flight attendant came by counting the passengers he asked her, "Excuse me, but does this train go to Tuesday?" She forgot the passenger count. The next time she came by he pointed to the empty seat next to him and asked, "Did you count my nephew? And when you have time, could you get him a glass of water?" She lost it again! The third time she wasn't to be tricked, and writing the passenger count down, she plonked herself down beside Erickson and asked, "How's your nephew feeling now?" To which Erickson replied, "Oh, just fine. He loves it when a pretty girl sits on his lap." Years later, he was in a much larger plane and was asked to help with a difficult passenger. He complied, and as the flight attendant accompanied him back to his seat, she stated, "By the way, Dr. Erickson, this train does go to Tuesday!"

We have become so involved with the technology of modern clinical practice—computers, the Internet, and so forth—that it is easy to underestimate the effect of the gentle art of conversation. We humans love to talk, gossip, share experiences, jokes, and stories. Who hasn't had the personal experience of feeling glum, perhaps for a good reason, and then a friend or partner arrives, and we begin to talk together. The conversation itself helps to shift our mood from inward brooding about our circumstances to a more outward, relating, social focus.

Setting the Mood

Clearly, clients don't consult us simply for a social chat, but I notice again and again that spending a few minutes socializing early in treatment can make a big difference later. To ask clients about their problem after asking about their relaxation activities is very different from starting straight into the problem-solving mode. By beginning the session with a conversation treating the client as a person, a relationship of normality and caring can be established and can provide a way of holding the problem, of containing it, together. This can be helpful and healing in itself.

We are all aware of iatrogenic illness (illness created by treatment) and the problems of drug interactions, but have we overlooked the harm we can do with our words? We can inadvertently turn something into a problem that a client was already handling well, for instance, when we tell the client that he or she is fixed, unchangeable, or that there is no possibility of change. Or, while trying to help clients, we invalidate them or convince them that we, not the client, are the expert. Milton Erickson stated, "While I have read a number of articles on this subject of iatrogenic disease, and have heard many discussions about it, there is one topic on which I haven't seen much written about and that is iatrogenic health. Iatrogenic health is a most important consideration—much more important than iatrogenic illness" (1981).

What we say, how we say it, how we set the mood for what we say with our clients are all crucial here. We can literally harm or heal with our words, the moods we create, and the conversations we foster.

There has been much concern expressed about the crisis in clinical practice, about the growing popularity of "alternative" practitioners. Could it be that what our clients are looking for isn't a sounding board, isn't us wisely saying, "Uh huh" or "I hear what you are saying," but rather someone who will treat them like human beings, reminding them that we are one of them, and that, together with some support from us, they can manage what seems at the time to be overwhelming and impossible to manage? Perhaps they are simply looking for a fellow human being who can help them to get their feet back on the ground of normal living, with its ups and downs, its joys and sorrows, its gains and losses—to rejoin the community of what Freud called "us ordinary neurotics."

Creating "Customer" Clients

Have you ever had the experience of trying sincerely to help clients with some personal, relationship, or family problem, and even though they have made the effort of making and keeping an appointment, the counseling conversation seems to be bogged down in layers of mud or snow? Nothing is moving, no matter what you try. Even worse, things may be going backwards! The client is becoming frustrated or bored; we are becoming frustrated or resentful.

At such a time, it is tempting to begin to doubt the sincerity of clients. Do they get some secondary gain and not really want to resolve their problem? It can also be tempting to doubt our own abilities. Should we have done more counseling training, read more articles or books? Should we retrain as a psychiatrist, so that then we would know?

There can be no doubt that although some clients have at least some ambivalence about giving up their problem, and at least some of us doing the counseling could have more skills, in many cases there is another option open to us to enhance the effectiveness of the counseling conversation and at the same time add to our personal and professional satisfaction. Steve de Shazer writes in *Clues: Investigating Solutions in Brief Therapy* (1988) about the trap of assuming that every client who comes for counseling is actively and responsibly ready to work on his or her problem. Those who are he labels *customers;* those who are not he labels *complainants* or *visitors.* In my own practice and in teaching counselors in this approach, I have learned that not recognizing that a client is a visitor or a complainant is a major, if not *the* major source of suffering, ineffectiveness, and professional burnout for anyone working in the counseling field.

Negotiating a "Customer"

Engaging clients in the counseling process, negotiating with clients so they can become engaged, can be rewarding. It may take only a few minutes and may allow the conversation to move on toward a solution. But without the preliminary steps, we could get bogged down in mutual frustration, and resignation can quickly set in.

A typical "visitor" is a teenager who, when asked "Why are you here?" replies with an infuriating "I don't know," possibly followed by "Can you smoke here?" or "Have we finished yet?" A typical "complainant" recognizes and complains bitterly about the reality and suffering produced by the problem, but experiences the solution as outside the self, with others. A typical "customer" freely acknowledges that there is a problem and then expresses a willingness to work to find a solution. Unless we find a way of influencing a client who presents as a complainant or a visitor, there is no solution to find:

Client	Problem	Solution	Our Response
Visitor	No	No	Frustration
Complainant	Yes	No	Inadequacy
Customer	Yes	Yes	Mutual liking

Nasrudin was down on his hands and knees under a street light when his long-suffering neighbor happened along and asked him what he was doing. "Looking for my house key" was Nasrudin's reply. So the neighbor, being the long-suffering person that he was, got down on his knees to help. After some time, when no key had been found, the neighbor asked, "Are you sure you dropped your key here?" "Oh, no," said Nasrudin, "I dropped it over there!" "But if you dropped it over there, then why are we looking for it here?" asked the by now exasperated neighbor. "I thought it would be obvious," said Nasrudin. "The light is better here!"

How often do we produce ineffectiveness in our search and exasperation in the process because, like the Mullah Nasrudin, we look in places that are familiar or comfortable for us, rather than where there is at least a chance of finding a solution?

A Visitor

A client who presents as a visitor has no personal investment in the process of looking for a solution to the problem. In fact, he or she does not perceive that there even *is* a problem.

The client has typically been sent by an agency, an employer, a spouse, a parent, or other. Further, some courts are mandating counseling as an alternative to a prison term, and some clients opt for counseling as a way of avoiding prison. When we try to engage such clients in useful conversation, they are usually bored and disinterested. We often find ourselves getting frustrated with these clients. Sometimes, I notice that I feel like shaking them. I haven't actually done so yet, nor do I expect to, but my reaction is one that I have found useful to alert me to someone "just visiting."

When encountering a visitor, de Shazer recommends that we first join the client in his or her individual worldview and then attempt to engage the client by asking for minimal changes that will be sufficient for the sender to stop sending the client to such a boring experience.

Joining.   Create a mood of general agreement to affirm the experience of the client:

❖ Yes, parents (teachers, wives, husbands, etc.) can be like that, can't they?

❖ Doesn't it aggravate you? Isn't it annoying when (the sender) tries to be so helpful?

❖ I've had that happen and hate it too. I can relate to that.

❖ It must be (a negative experience: boring, annoying, etc.) to have to come here.

Engaging.   Help clients determine the minimum they must do to stop coming for counseling. What will satisfy the sender, the client, *and* the counselor? If a set number of sessions have been ordered, perhaps by a court, the counselor could say, "Given that we have to do time together, how can we best use the time?"

A 14-year-old boy was referred by his father because of the father's dissatisfaction with the boy's school results. When I asked the lad why he was here, after a few obligatory "I dunno's," he eventually told me about his father's problem. The way he spoke, it was obvious that to him, the problem was his father's and that he didn't have any problem at all, beyond the inconvenience of having to waste time talking to me. I noticed some impatience on my part, and, coupled with his stating that his father had sent him, I was alerted to his behaving like a visitor. I immediately validated the legitimacy of his position: to join him and not become another in a long list of people who were his enemies, I said, "Fathers are like that. They worry about their kids' performance. My father used to get on my back, I get on my kids' backs, and maybe you'll get on your kids' backs when you grow up and have kids of your own."

He relaxed noticeably and looked relieved and a little amused that an adult, usually appearing as an alien life form, was actually speaking his kind of language. This allowed me to move to the next step of engaging him by asking, "What's the least you can do to get your father off your back so he'll stop sending you here? You'll probably have to do something, otherwise he'll keep making you come back and talk this kind of boring talk. If he doesn't send you here, he may send you somewhere else, maybe even worse! So what do you think you can get away with? What's the smallest change you can make?"

He thought for a moment, then offered the idea that perhaps if he did some homework regularly that might help, because his father was always nagging him about not doing enough. I then asked him about the least amount that would satisfy his father. He thought two hours might do it, and when I asked him if he could get away with one, he didn't think so.

One and a half might be okay, so we settled for one and a half. I asked if he thought his father would expect him to work on Sunday night, and he thought probably not; the same with Saturday night. When I asked about Friday, he thought he probably wouldn't be able to get away without doing some. I could then propose that he try doing one and a half hours of homework on Monday to Friday evenings and see if that would keep his father happy. He even agreed to return in a week to report back to me about his progress.

A week later he was pleased to inform me that his father was already easing off and giving him a bit more space. This prompted me to ask if he thought this meant that he might be able to cut his homework down to an hour, but he didn't think this would be acceptable. He readily accepted that an hour and a half of homework on those five nights was worth it to have some relief from all the hassles his father had given him. He was glad to have his father off his case. I imagine that the father was also relieved to see his son doing at least some work.

The conversation is designed so that there is no call for responsibility from visitors. They can hardly be expected to be willing to give much because in their view, they don't actually have a problem. It is a personal and professional pleasure to see results from what would normally be considered an aggressive, uncooperative client.

A Complainant

When clients present as complainants, they recognize that there is a problem, but they believe the solution lies with others. Even though the problem is acknowledged and is usually painfully present, looking for a solution within the client will be pointless. As long as clients place their own efforts on hold until there is a change of weather, government, work practices, or whatever, they will be waiting, and there will be no chance of progress.

When we try to engage such clients in useful conversation, they are usually resentful, aggressive, and frustrated. And we often get frustrated with ourselves, feeling inadequate. Sometimes, I notice that I am silently berating myself for not studying more, not going to more workshops on counseling, or, in the extreme, contemplating a career change—usually landscape gardening, in my case. My reaction is one that I have found useful to alert me to the presence of a complainant.

Steve de Shazer recommends that after we join complainant clients in their individual worldview, we offer them a compliment. This must be heard as sincere to avoid clients feeling patronized, which would only add insult to injury. Only then should we attempt to engage them by asking for some small change that they can make to lessen their suffering, however minimally.

I find no difficulty offering a compliment and making it sincere by placing myself in the client's shoes and imagining how the situation would be for me. I find that often I am amazed at the client's resilience in the face of all he or she has suffered. Frequently, clients are so relieved after this conversation that at last someone is willing to openly acknowledge the reality and validity of their suffering, that they weep openly with tears of relief and gratitude.

Joining and Complimenting. Acknowledge the client's worldview, then offer a *sincere* compliment:

- ❖ Seems to me that you're handling things quite well.

- ❖ Given what you've had to put up with, I'm surprised at how well you are doing.

- ❖ I can imagine that some may think you're doing surprisingly well.

- ❖ It must be awful to have that happen.

❖ I'm not sure I could have handled it as well as you have.

❖ You've probably had more pain in the last week than I expect to have in my lifetime.

Engaging.   Encourage "I" responses to promote ownership/authorship:

❖ What could *you* do so they wouldn't do that?

❖ How could *you* do something different?

❖ What could *we* do?

❖ How could you change the other person's behavior?

❖ If you could do something, the smallest possible thing, what might it be?

A woman in her early 80s was referred for help with her relentless back pain resulting from severe osteoporosis and compression fracture of L2. She was accompanied by her only slightly younger sister. They both looked desperate. The pain was bad enough, but she was not able to tolerate pain-relieving medication. They both complained about the pain. They spoke as though the pain were separate from the sufferer and beyond her control and the control of her physicians.

I noticed that although she was clearly suffering a very real problem, she was looking outside of herself for the solution. This is the requirement for a diagnosis of "complainant." I also noticed my own reaction of feeling somewhat inadequate in the face of her suffering and lack of relief to date. This reaction confirmed my diagnosis. I told her, "You have been through hell. The amount of pain you have suffered . . . it's really terrible [joining]. I am amazed at the way you are coping as well as you are, given the severity of the pain, and the lack of help from medication [joining and compliment]."

She was silent, then tears began to form in the corner of her eyes—her sister's also. She looked relieved and peaceful, as if she had been heard for the first time. Most of us are too uncomfortable to be helpless in the presence of suffering. We want to either help or leave. Her emotion was palpable, and led into our inquiring together about small changes she could make: how she could avoid activities that exacerbated her pain; how she could think about a TV program she enjoyed while she walked to keep herself active (previously, she had walked willingly, but the first steps were very painful to her); and instead of going to bed dreading the pain, she could find pleasant memories to occupy her mind as she drifted off to sleep.

Her response was as subtle as it was dramatic. A small change allowed some return of hope—something that had been missing from her life. These changes could be found only after those preliminary steps in the conversation—joining and complimenting—so she could look to her own capacities, having had the legitimacy of her dilemma validated.

ASSESSING THE PROBLEM AND FINDING A SOLUTION

What Is a Problem?

Clients consult us because they have problems of some sort. In a counseling situation, clients want to talk with us about how to get help to deal with a personal issue: some unwanted emotional reaction such as fear, sadness, or anger; how to cope with a relationship, find a new relationship, break from an old relationship, stay in an existing relationship; or perhaps some difficulty related to work, such as too much work, not enough work, no work at all, lack of appreciation on the job, job insecurity, difficulty dealing with a subordinate, a boss, the CEO, and so on. Clients want counseling to help resolve their problems.

In our everyday clinical practice, we often need to ask about when the problem began and what makes it worse. We may want to look for the cause so we can then make a diagnosis and formulate a treatment plan.

In counseling conversations this may not always be necessary. Some problems can begin at a specific time for a specific reason, and long after that situation has passed the problem continues. A senior high student can begin to bite her nails before her final exams, and 10 years later, she is simply trying to remove jagged edges. The exams are long gone, but the problem persists; it can be self-perpetuating. Someone may sleep poorly after a specific upset: a child's illness, the loss of a parent. Long after the precipitating cause has passed, the sleeplessness can continue or even worsen. Trying to go to sleep or worrying about the result of not sleeping then becomes the cause of the insomnia; in this case, seeking the cause will be unhelpful and may even make the situation worse. The client wants to know *how to go to sleep,* not *why he or she is awake.* In such cases, the counseling conversation may require that we shift our approach from looking for the cause of the problem to looking more immediately in the direction of a solution.

So, what is it about a problem that makes it a problem?

Many problems are problems because of our expectations and interpretations of the circumstances and not in the circumstances themselves. Different individuals experience the same circumstances very differently, depending on their individual values and beliefs.

Viktor Frankl, the originator of logotherapy, which emphasizes our human necessity to make meaning out of experiences, wrote about an elderly man who came to him at his clinic. He told Frankl that he, too, was a doctor and that since the death of his wife two years previously, he had suffered from severe depression. He said he loved her above all else. Rather than giving him advice, Frankl asked, "What would have happened if you had died first, and your wife would have had to survive you?" He said right away that this would have caused her tremendous suffering. Frankl replied, "You see, you have saved your wife from that terrible suffering. You have spared her this suffering, at the price that you have to survive and mourn her." The client said nothing, but shook Frankl's hand and calmly left the office. This conversation allowed the widower to totally shift his experience. His depression was not only alleviated, it was removed totally.

When Counseling Works, What Is It That Works?

A study by Garfield and Bergin (1994) examining the cause of success in counseling revealed that the benefits could be categorized as follows:

- ❖ 40% extracounseling factors (i.e., nothing to do with the counseling at all!).

- ❖ 30% counseling relationship factors: rapport, humanity, understanding, empathy.

- ❖ 15% hope for future was produced in the counseling process.

- ❖ 15% counseling technique employed.

It can be a shock to see that technique is so small a factor, and yet this is the area that tends to be emphasized both in our training and in practice:

A couple had been making slow progress in couples counseling to resolve their problem of not being able to share a bed since a heated argument several months previously. They could each acknowledge their contributions to the problem and were gradually getting around to forgiving each other, but they couldn't seem to make the move back to the shared bed. Late one Saturday afternoon, some friends called in unexpectedly from out of town, stayed for a meal and on into the evening. Late at night the question arose: Where should the visitors sleep? There were no motels nearby, so it was decided that they should stay the night. But where should they sleep? If the guests used the spare bedroom, their hosts would have to share the main bedroom. With some reluctance, they agreed together that this was best, and by the morning, there had been a lot worked through. They were able to complete their couples counseling at the next session.

The counseling may have helped to set the mood for change, but the change itself came from a place totally outside the counseling conversation. We can see, then, that sometimes we can look immediately toward a solution without first having to follow the detour of looking for the cause.

How Can We Get to a Solution?

When clients experience a problem, they report about the problem as if it is there 60 seconds of every minute, 60 minutes of every hour, and 24 hours of every day. They unintentionally fill in the gaps between the problem times as if there are no times when they are free of the problem. One way to get clients thinking about a solution to their problem is to question them about a time when the problem was not bothering them and then help them to reach that state again.

Solution-Oriented Questioning

It can be useful to ask our clients questions such as "What is it like when the problem is not there?" or "What is different when it is not so severe?" This can help to direct the client's attention to what is working that he or she may have overlooked. We can then ask, "If you wanted to have more of these problem-free times, how could you do that?"

A couple requested counseling because they were arguing "all the time" and wanted to put a stop to it. I asked them, "What do you do when you are not arguing?" After looking at each other for a moment, they realized that they were then more accepting that their partner might be at least partly right and they themselves may be partly wrong. When I followed by asking "If you wanted more times like this, how could you get them?" they looked thoughtful again, and between them decided that it would be helpful to remind themselves anytime there was an argument in the air that both were partly right and partly wrong. They returned a week later to report that life had settled and there were now just the ordinary disagreements to be expected. I only had to congratulate them on finding such an elegant and useful solution and send them on their way satisfied and more in control of their own relationship, with their shared solution built into their future.

We have all been in a situation where, if someone offers us answers or advice, we are not likely to take much notice. But because the couple came up with the solution themselves, it was their solution, so they could own it and use it. This approach focuses on generating with clients a workable solution they can create themselves and begin to live with, instead of spending scarce and expensive time looking for the root of the problem.

When counselors first try this approach, they are sometimes concerned that they are avoiding the "real" problem, or that they are dealing with the problem only superficially. Clients, on the other hand, are often grateful and delighted that they were able to deal with their problem in such a time- and cost-effective manner. They are relieved to discover that their situation was not as severe as they had dreaded it may have been.

Stating the Concern

Some opinions grip tighter than others. We may be willing to concede on some issues, but others are not open for negotiation. Core values such as "Torture is evil," "Cruelty to children is never acceptable," and "My children will never go hungry" feel as if they are so deeply held that removing them would remove us—conceding would kill us.

The closer the concern or belief is to our core, the more it has the potential to allow other changes to occur around it. Stating the concern and making it apparent is affirming the *being* of the client and allows the therapy conversation to move in a different direction—one with more opportunities and choices.

Sometimes in a counseling conversation, we want to change the circumstances: the actions a client is taking, the

---

SOLUTION-ORIENTED QUESTIONS

❖ What improvements have you noticed since you made the appointment?

❖ When does the problem bother you least?

❖ How will you know that you've overcome this difficulty?

❖ Who will be most surprised when you are OK again?

❖ Where will you be when you first notice how good you are feeling?

surroundings, aspects of the therapist-client relationship, or work conditions. At other times, when there is a stuckness about the process of trying to change—a client wants to change, tries to change, suffers in the process, and yet change doesn't happen—some other approach is called for. Trying to change what is not open to change is like trying to make one-self understood in a foreign country by speaking louder: not very helpful. In these situations, we can accept the client's experience that change isn't happening, validate the legiti-macy of this, and look with the client for what concern may be keeping the problem stuck as a problem. Stating that con-cern, legitimizing the concern, congratulating the client for being the kind of person who would have such a concern can allow the circumstances to remain peacefully, safe from at-tempts to change them at the expense of the important belief or concern, and all can yet be well.

Problem states are characterized by a paucity of options, solution states by a wide choice of options. Our job as coun-selors is to bring increased options to our clients. Giving up on trying to change the unchangeable is a wonderful option to many clients and can afford us much relief also.

Reframing

Humberto Maturana in *The Tree of Knowledge* (1988) said, "Everything said is said by an observer." What we observe is profoundly influenced by our point of observation, previ-ous experience, expectations, point of view, and prejudices, to name a few. Although they are intricately interrelated, we can distinguish among what is being observed, the observer that we are, and the observations we make. We can say that a problem is experienced as such because of the "frame" within which the circumstances are experienced. A way to resolve a problem, then, is to shift the frame: to reframe it.

When Tom Sawyer said that it's not every day you get a chance to paint a fence, he not only removed the problem frame, but his friends were soon paying him for the privilege! When my car had a dead battery, it was a problem to me because it interrupted my plans, but to the supplier of new batteries it would be a problem if this did not occur. We have all had experiences when a problem suddenly disappeared when viewed differently; for example, an argument with a loved one becomes an opportunity to make up; a child's broken toy becomes an opportunity to spend time with Dad while he fixes it.

When clients experience a problem there is an emotion (a concern) in the background to which they are usually blind. Asking "What is the concern?" can shift the mood from self-blame or frustration to adequacy or possibility and allow new actions to appear. Imagine a client who complains of feeling guilty. Because guilt can appear as a problem only if there is some background concern about morality, to reply that the client must be a highly moral person can produce a delightful interruption of the previous mood of conflict:

A young man suffering from depression came for counseling following the death of his estranged father and talked about his regret at not speaking with him before he died. He said that there were so many things he wanted to say, but now it was too late. He said he was sorry that he hadn't made the effort to visit his father in the hospital when he knew he was dying. I listened for what I could hear in the background of this man's experience as he spoke with me, and I heard regret and guilt. I was then able to comment, "Your relationship with your father must have been more important than you realized. And about your guilt: you must have high moral standards about this, or you wouldn't be suffering so deeply." He looked stunned, as if he had just seen something important, and then began to cry tears of relief as he recognized just how important that was. His recognition didn't provide an opportunity to speak with his dead father, but it did resolve his conflict and he was peaceful about it. His regret and guilt had been dispersed, dissolved in our conversation together. The whole process took less than 20 minutes.

"I'm guilty" is a comment from a person who is highly moral. As we've noted, to offer the response "You must be a highly moral person" shifts the mood from conflict and doubt, which are natural but not helpful moods, to solidness and wholeness, which can be surprising and very welcome:

A mother consulted me because she was concerned about her 14-year-old son's behavior. He was uncooperative at home and difficult at school, and she had received complaints from teachers and other parents. She was losing sleep and wanted to talk about her problem. She wondered about taking sleeping tablets or even antidepressants. She looked down, with a frown on her face, her shoulders slumped forward, and told the story in scattered fragments, requiring some mental agility from me just to follow her train of thought.

She was worried about her son, his future, her adequacy as a mother. I affirmed her reaction, reassuring her that any mother would be worried about a son in this kind of situation. She relaxed somewhat. I then told her that the worrying she was doing, the suffering she was in about her son, was direct evidence of her concern for her son. "It is because you are a conscientious, concerned, caring mother that you are upset like this. Less caring mothers wouldn't be so concerned about a son and his future."

Her mood changed dramatically. Her eyes glistened, her face relaxed, she sat back in the chair, and she looked me in the eye for the first time. "So I'm not a bad mother?" It was a relief for her to hear that and feel that, and we then could

*begin to discuss ways that she could set solid limits, be as flex-
ible as possible, and begin to deal with the situation.*

*Her son appeared a week later, sent by his mother, and was
a typical "visitor." I joined with his mood by agreeing with
him that coming to see me must be boring and annoying, and
reminded him that boring though it may be, his mother had
sent him and would probably continue to send him until she
saw some change. I asked him what he thought was the smallest change his mother would be satisfied with. What would be
the least he could do, so she would stop sending him to me, or
maybe someone even worse? He thought that if he did some
homework most nights that this might suffice. He thought that
he might be able to get away with an hour.*

*He agreed to return a week later to report on whether he
had been able to get away with one hour's homework, and he
said that his mother was "off his case" and he was pretty
pleased about that. I noticed that he was reactive to being told
what to do (he was 14), and considering the idea of what concern might be in the background of his "problem" with authority, I asked him if he might be the kind of person who
valued his individuality. He looked pleased as he agreed that
his individuality was the most important thing in his life. We
were beginning to get on just fine. We then spoke together
about the difficult challenge of maintaining individuality and
being a member of a group. We discussed how he could play
his own style of basketball and still stay on the team. It was a
useful conversation for both of us.*

When I reflect on the pivotal points in my conversations
with the mother and the son, they seemed to occur when I
was able to state their concern: for the mother, a concern
about her son's future; for the son, about his individuality.
When each heard the statement, they could hardly disagree,
because for the problem to be a problem, the concern must
have been there in the background somewhere.

REFRAMING PROBLEMS AS CONCERNS	
Problem	**Concern**
I'm anxious.	Personal security is important to you.
I'm stressed out.	Taking care of yourself is important to you.
I'm depressed.	You want to be happy.
I'm feeling suicidal.	The quality of your life is crucial to you.
I'm worried about the possibility of being made redundant.	You are someone who values security in your future.
I shout at my kids.	Quality mothering and your children's emotional well-being are important to you.
I can't manage my time.	Organization and responsibility are important to you.
I don't want to talk about my problem.	Privacy is important to you. You want to do justice to your problem.
I'm broke due to gambling.	Providing for your family is important to you.
I'm not sure I still love my husband.	You are determined to be genuine about your relationship.
I am having trouble leaving the relationship, even though I know I have to.	You want to do the right thing by yourself and your partner.
My teacher is an idiot.	You need to be treated respectfully. Realizing your potential is important to you.

Reframing the problem as an expression of a background concern doesn't imply agreement or support for the problem. It doesn't change any of the components of the problem. What it can sometimes do is allow for the ground of the problem to shift, so the context changes and the mood can be transformed. The client who was feeling defective and a lesser being in the problem mood can shift to being a whole and adequate and concerned being who will then be more able to deal with the circumstances of the problem and get into the activity of managing it.

This reframing can be a powerful, empowering conversation that can allow for a different being, a different set and availability of resources to appear in the client. Sometimes, reframing can be sufficient to resolve the problem totally; other circumstances require something more. Reframing changes permanently the ground supporting the problem. If further counseling is needed, it can proceed with a client who is on solid human ground, rather than shaky, defective problem ground.

Summary

Martin Heidegger uses the word *Dasein* in his inquiry into the question of what kind of being the human being is. *Dasein* is translated as "being-in-the-world," so that the "being" and "the world" that the being is in are not separable. Humans are concerned beings. Because our hand is part of us, when our hand hurts, we are concerned about it. When something happens to our child, our partner, our client, we are concerned. Heidegger points to concerns as central to humanness, and so it is hardly strange that in any problem, some concern will be there, not far in the background, generating the problem as a problem, driving the problem toward resolution.

By stating clients' concerns, we affirm their legitimacy as valid human beings, doing the best they can in the situation they are in. As a consequence of validating them, we help to validate their potential to deal with their life circumstances. In working with clients to assist them to resolve their problems, it makes perfect sense that we examine their concerns: by identifying these concerns and bringing them into the foreground of our conversational experience, we place ourselves in the middle of human interactions, ones that will be pivotal for change. By identifying the concern and stating it, we reframe the situation: instead of a defective client suffering a problem, we see a whole and good human being who then is more able to manage a situation.

THE ART OF THE QUESTION

The most challenging aspect of solution-oriented therapy is knowing the right questions to ask. We tend to think change has to be difficult and requires extensive exploration and deep understanding. Sometimes change does require this, and sometimes it doesn't. What is amazing is the powerful simplicity of asking the right question to effect a change in the client. A simple, well-timed question can be the catalyst for a small change that the client, with our support, can allow to develop and so head toward resolving the problem. If the client wants to change, the questions counselors ask can help the client to initiate and consolidate change with minimal direction and encouragement:

A woman with severe pain in her neck, shoulders, and arms after a whiplash injury was referred to me for pain management. I asked her what she did to make her pain less severe. She said she achieved this when she paced herself by doing as much exercise as she could cope with to extend her range of movement without pushing too hard. When she could challenge herself gently she was comfortable. I encouraged her to pay attention to how much she pushed herself, and to keep a balance between the challenge and overdoing it. I encouraged her to do what worked and she found it helpful.

✦ Presuppositional Questions

The questions we ask influence the answers we get, and the answers we get influence the outcome for our clients. Imagine a man in traction in the hospital because of a fractured femur. The bone is healing well, but he is far from comfortable. He is watching his favorite team's first playoff game in years on television and they are ahead toward the end of the final quarter. Just as the other team looks like they might catch up, the nurse on her rounds asks the client, "How's your leg?" What do you think happens to his experience of his pain? It is likely that the pain appears in response to the well-meaning inquiry. What do you think happens when the nurse leaves and he becomes involved in the TV again? The other team misses the goal. The final buzzer sounds. His team is victorious. How much pain would the man feel at this moment?

When clients arrive for a session, how we greet them can make a difference to the outcome of the session. If we ask, "How's the problem?" or a more neutral "How have you been?" the result can be different from asking "What improvements have you noticed since last time?" The latter question puts clients into a solution mood and requires that they begin to look within the experiences of improvement, rather than looking at whether there have been improvements. Such a small difference in the greeting can take the rest of the session in a different direction.

"How's the problem?" is likely to lead to a conversation about the problem. Even if the client arrived feeling okay, asking this question can unwittingly aggravate the problem. "How have you been?" allows for a report on the good and bad of the experiences related to the problem area. "What improvements have you seen?" and "What else needs to happen to make you feel better?" get clients thinking about a solution. Following these kinds of questions, the results are more likely to be owned by the clients, so they are then empowered to cope with other issues:

A couple who had been arguing returned for their second consultation after being given some homework to notice what works for them and pay attention to what they are doing when things are working out. I asked them what was happening when things were going well. They looked at each other, and the storm clouds passed as they smiled sheepishly. They began to report about the way they were finding activities they could share: watching TV, going for a walk on the weekend, going to the movies—nothing spectacular, but the result was obvious. The previous battling was being supplanted by the experience of being together. They were beginning to share activities as they had years before, and the fighting became a temporary part of their relationship that they were keen to put behind them. I shared with them an episode of fighting my wife and I got into a few years previously about two wire coat hangers. I wanted to keep them in case they came in handy, and my wife wanted to throw them out. We managed to shout at each other for more than an hour before the absurdity hit home. The memory of that episode has been invaluable in defusing other situations: we can say "coat hangers" and begin laughing. It is impossible to fight after that memory.

DESIGNING PRESUPPOSITIONAL QUESTIONS		
Statement	Yes/No Question	Presuppositional Question
This is a good book.	Is this a good book?	What is good about this book for you?
You can use the material in this book.	Can you use the material in this book?	Which material in this book will it be easiest for you to use?
Some of your clients are more difficult than others.	Are some of your clients more difficult than others?	What can you observe about your easier clients that you can bring to your more difficult clients?
You are happy.	Are you happy?	When you are happy, what's different for you?
You are learning.	Are you learning?	What helps you to learn best?

The Miracle Question

We have seen how useful it can be to inquire about changes that have already begun to happen before the current appointment, previous examples of getting over similar problems in the past, and occasions when the problem has been absent without its absence being noticed. For clients to discover early in the session that they are already doing something helpful is empowering, and makes continuing these activities easier for them. For example, if clients can recall getting over a previous bout of depression, a previous loss, or a previous crisis of whatever sort, it can encourage them that this crisis can also be overcome. For a client to discover ② that there actually are times when the problem isn't there or isn't as severe can provide a new sense of hope when the client is feeling hopeless. A new chance for the client to pursue options when previously there seemed to be none can seem close to miraculous, as well as being a tremendously satisfying experience for the counselor.

But what if our best joint efforts don't produce these responses? What if the client says, "There haven't been any changes since making the appointment," or "I've never had this problem before," or "There isn't any time when the problem's not there or less troublesome—it's always there, it's always bad, and I don't see how it can ever be any different"? Because clients have a recurrent tendency to behave like themselves, some won't be able to identify any preappointment changes, some won't be able to recall how they overcame similar problems previously, and some won't be able to notice any times when the problem isn't there—they will say not even for a second, not even when they are asleep!

Am I the only one who has faced a particularly difficult counseling situation and felt so stuck that I think "This would take a miracle"? I'm not only talking about the client with multiple or chronic problems, or the client whose name on the afternoon list makes your heart sink as you groan silently and think "Oh no!" We all get stuck sometimes, as do our clients, but when a miracle seems what's needed, where can we go? Miracles are out of fashion with the deep cynicism and disconnection of our postmodern society. Instead of wondering why we ever went into this work, or contemplating a career change, we can allow our sweaty palms and palpitating heart to subside from near panic. When the situation seems so impossible that we find ourselves thinking

"I need a miracle here," we can begin to wonder about whether a miracle might be available.

If it feels as if a miracle is needed, why not ask for one? This shift in direction moves client and therapist from a shared experience of frustration and impotence to a focus on the client's wishes and resources—from what hasn't worked in the past to what might work in the future. The focus shifts from problem and deficit to resourcefulness, from stuckness to new actions, from the past to the future, from resignation to possibility. Steve de Shazer recommends that at such apparent dead ends in the counseling conversation, we purposely ask what would be different if a miracle actually did happen.

THE MIRACLE QUESTION

❖ You've had this problem for some time now, and in spite of all your efforts, it's persisting. I wonder what it would be like if, when you were asleep tonight, a miracle happened and the problem just disappeared. Because it happened while you were asleep, you wouldn't need to remember just how it happened, but you would know that the problem was gone. What would be different when you woke in the morning?

❖ Even though you have tried unsuccessfully to re-solve your problem, if you could find a way to have things the way you want, what would that be like?

❖ If something special were to happen, what would you like it to be?

The result of asking this question can seem almost miraculous. For many chronic sufferers, the problem is so much a part of their everyday life that they can become resigned to it and give up hope of ever getting over it. Asking the miracle question can sometimes reawaken that hope or reopen the possibility of life after the problem. Even if the question doesn't elicit any immediate response, we, as experts, have seriously spoken about that prospect, and the client has to at least contemplate the possibility of saying good-bye to the problem, even if ultimately rejecting it. The pristine quality of the problem is sullied to some degree, its impregnability begins to show cracks and can never be quite as certain in the future. This means that the question can be useful even if there isn't an immediate benefit.

Sometimes when we ask a version of the miracle question, the answer is so unrealistic that its relevance may not be immediately apparent. But my Irish ancestors used to say "If you don't know where you're going, you may just end up in a different place" and "If you don't know where you're going, any road will take you there." When clients find themselves sinking into the swamps of despair, it's easy for us to feel the downward pull also, so finding a way out of the bog is helpful to everyone.

That Really Would Be a Miracle!

A professional woman was becoming overwhelmed by her diminishing counseling practice and doubted her ability to continue more than several more months. Bills to pay, promotion of her practice—it all seemed too much. We agreed that a miracle was needed.

When I asked her what would be different if suddenly all her problems were solved, she became animated and said she could retire, buy a house in the country, go overseas for an extended vacation, and shop for a new wardrobe. She described something that sounded unrealistic to me. So I asked her further about what would be different for her if all that happened. She looked pensive and peaceful as she reflected that she had not taken a holiday for more than seven years, rarely had time off on weekends, had given up going out with her husband because she had allowed herself to become so weighed down with the burden of it all.

This provided an opportunity for us to inquire about what small beginnings she could make. She decided she could go out dancing with her husband perhaps once a month. She could take a weekend off occasionally. I asked what else she could do that would nourish her without adding to her financial burden. Perhaps she could walk in the botanical gardens, along the beach, or visit friends in the country?

This conversation caused a profound shift in her mood. She lost the burden in front of my eyes and began to plan in a realistic way how she could do some of these simple things. Over the next few months, she altered her counseling schedule so she had days off, some of which she used to clarify what she was good at and what interested her in her practice. This helped her to market herself more clearly. Asking the miracle question didn't create a miracle, but it helped her to see realistically what had been missing for her so she could begin to take care of it and herself.

Even if the answer to the miracle question is unrealistic, it can help to clarify a direction for change and to encourage sharing between counselor and client, fostering the relationship and allowing trust to develop. This clarity, communication, and trust can be a major help in difficult situations. Having some relief (ours as well as our clients') can prevent burnout and add to the experience of satisfaction in our work.

BRINGING COUNSELING TO LIFE

We have looked at ways of creating rapport with our clients by asking them about their hobbies and spare time activities. This can help to generate a mood of equality and humanity in the beginning of the counseling session. We noted that talking about hobbies creates an atmosphere of pleasure and ordinariness so that when we begin to discuss the problem, it is often experienced as more manageable. If we then ask about the problem from the perspective of what it is about the problem that the client wants to change, it can help to focus the conversation in a useful direction and add to the effectiveness of and mutual satisfaction with the therapy process.

We discovered the value of asking clients about any changes they may have already noticed or begun to make, and that as a result, they sometimes discover that they are already beginning to move down the solution track. Our work then is to encourage and support them as they continue down that path.

Milton Erickson was a major proponent of these tactics and illustrated this when he spoke about his experience of returning from high school one afternoon to find a horse in his family's yard, saddled and obviously hot and bothered. He cornered the horse, gave it a drink, climbed into the saddle, and said "Giddyap." When they reached the road, the young Erickson allowed the horse to decide which way to turn, and when the horse wanted to stop and nibble on the grass on the roadside, Erickson said his job was to remind the horse that the road was where they were supposed to be. Several miles down the road, the horse trotted into a farmyard, where the farmer said, "So that's where the critter got to! How did you know to bring it back here?" To which Erickson replied, "I didn't, but I knew the horse did." That's how counseling should proceed.

We have also investigated asking clients about the times when the problem isn't there—the times in between the problem time—when they are actually experiencing more of what they want to experience (although our biology usually makes those times opaque to us so that we can't readily observe them). It can be a joy to remind our clients about those times and watch as their mood changes from heavy resignation or anxiety to a lighter, more optimistic sense of possibilities appearing over the horizon.

You may be starting to notice what you are already doing that is useful in a counseling session and to enjoy the results of extending that process even further. As counselors, we must also ask how the benefits, insights, understandings, and new actions that emerge in a session can be transferred to everyday life. How can the conversations in our office be translated into the clients' daily activities? This is a crucial question. Unless we can answer it, we won't be helping our clients with their actual life experiences, which are what brought them to counseling in the first place.

Between-Session Questions

One of the recurring dilemmas we face is when we have a useful, insightful counseling session, the client feels more hopeful, we feel pleased with the conversation, and the client returns a week later and seems to have lost the plot again. The soup of life has reclaimed the client and the client's resolve, new hopes are dissolved, and we are back where we started.

At least occasionally, a client returns and gladdens both our hearts by reporting new experiences, new interactions, new moods of possibility. This brings us to the question of how we can have more of the latter and less of the former. Hopes for change can sit like a New Year's resolution somewhere on the back shelves of our mind gathering the dust of guilt or despair. One way of bringing counseling into the client's life and ensuring that some change will actually happen is to assign homework activities that will direct clients' attention to formulating solutions to their problems.

When we ask clients to notice what they want to leave *un*changed, they can begin to look at their experience from a different perspective, in a different mood, and they may begin to appreciate some aspects of their experience that had been previously overlooked. Although this doesn't remove or solve the problem, it can help to restore a more normal balance to their life in general. At least occasionally, this can tip the scales back toward normality and start the slide toward solving their dilemma.

Asking clients to keep track of the times when things are going well can also help to shift their focus in a more helpful direction. "If you look for the evil in people, you will most certainly find it" translates into "If you look for the possibilities around you, there is at least a chance of seeing some of them."

Problems have such a predictability about them. They are like a bit of life that has got stuck in a groove, taking us round and round in the same place in a mood of resignation and hopelessness. When we ask our clients to notice what happens when they do something different, it can help to break the hypnotic spell the problem had on their behavior and let them see the bigger picture, perhaps for the first time in a while. We can add to the texture and relevance of the experience by asking further questions, such as "Who would be the first person to realize the change?" or "How would you know that he or she had realized it?" They are simple enough questions, but the value to our clients can be huge.

Earlier we learned that the most important factor in producing change in counseling, independent of the method of

Between-Session Questions and Homework Activities

❖ Notice what you want to leave unchanged, what you are already happy with.

❖ What is it about your partner that you love most?

❖ Notice what your partner says is your most endearing characteristic.

❖ Keep track of the times when things are going well.

❖ How can you make sure you don't let the good times slip past unnoticed?

❖ Which will be the smallest and easiest of these changes to pay attention to?

❖ Write down what happens when you do something different.

❖ Think about who would be the first person to realize something is different about you. How would you know that he or she had realized it?

❖ What will your partner's response be when he or she notices the change?

❖ How long will you need to allow your partner to realize that the changes are permanent?

❖ Which of these changes that you want will family notice before you do?

counseling used, is due to "client factors" (i.e., resulting from influences outside the counseling session), which account for a massive 40% of all change! The next most important influence (30%) is the counseling relationship leading to rapport and trust. Fifteen percent of the benefit is due to instilling a sense of hope for the future, and only 15% is due to the particular method of counseling used. These findings point to the importance of a future orientation in our counseling work and of ensuring that we generate a mood of trust and respect in our clients. These factors give direct access to 45% of the benefits for our clients.

By attending to the "client factors," we also have the possibility of adding another massive 40% to our clients' results. Asking questions such as the ones described earlier can lead us directly into this area. If we ask clients to notice what they want to leave unchanged, they may become pleasantly disoriented: from thinking only about what they wanted to change they begin to see what had been right under their nose, unseen because of its proximity and familiarity. It is easy to be unaware of our own little fingers until something, such as reading this, brings them to our attention.

By asking our clients to keep track of the times when things are going well, they begin to see with the eyes of a different observer, one who can see solutions and benefits that may have been there previously, but because the clients were stuck in a problem mode, they were unable to see them. This blindness to the obvious is something we know about from our anatomy. We all have a blind spot in our visual field, but we are blind to that blind spot: we fill in the gaps as if there were no gaps. Similarly, when we ask our clients to do something different, we assist them to interrupt their usual viewpoint and leave the way open to see what they had overlooked previously. We have all experienced driving a different way to work or traveling by train instead of car and been able to observe many different buildings, roads, and shops that previously were hidden to us. They had always been there, of course, but we could see them only when we were in a place where they could become visible.

Counselors are exhorted to follow the maxim *Primum non nocare:* First, do no harm. It can be a relief when we don't need to actually *do* a lot except help generate a mood that will allow our clients to get back on track—their track, not ours. By respectfully and gently encouraging them in the direction of their solution, all can be well, and we can all be satisfied. We know we aren't experts or all-powerful beings, and our clients know we aren't, so it can be a relief to give the power, the source of change, the ability to discover solutions and put them into action, back where they belong: with the client.

CHAPTER THREE

*Emotions and the
Body in Counseling*

As you read what follows, I again invite you to keep certain questions in mind: How does what I am reading relate to my experience, personal and professional? What observations have I already made similar to what I am reading? What is being overlooked here? How can I make use of what I am reading in my personal and professional life?

EMOTIONS: WHAT ARE THEY?

All humans are emotional beings, yet emotions seem so mysterious and often irrational—how could they not? In counseling, emotions have a special place. For some counselors, they are considered mandatory; for others, they are a nuisance.

Emotions have also served as signposts to hot spots in our clients' psyche. In a counseling session, if we notice a client's eyes are filling up or widening in fear we might ask "Is there something that's upsetting you about that?" and use the response as a signal about what the therapy should focus on next. Although all of these ideas can be useful, there is another understanding emerging.

We have already observed that when we consider language as concerned with more than describing an already existing reality, we can begin to influence future actions in our conversations together. If we look at emotions as domains of action or predispositions to action, we discover that emotions are another area that we cannot only observe, but use as a point of interaction to influence whole areas of action. Of course, generating rapport, including trust and respect, in the

53

therapeutic relationship is primary in allowing any effective change to begin.

One of the concerns I hear expressed in workshops when I am teaching counseling is that of abreaction in a client. What happens if there is repressed anger, fear, or sadness, and in the intimate experience of counseling, the client is able to release those emotions? In my experience, we don't need to fear any emotions that appear in counseling conversations any more than we need fear those emotions in everyday life. If someone cries, feels sad, angry, or fearful, what would we do in an ordinary situation? We would ask what we can do to help and do what we could that was useful and appropriate. As in life, so in counseling.

Emotions and Action

Rafael Echeverria (1994), inspired by Humberto Maturana, has made an important contribution to the study of emotions and action. They claim that emotions are predispositions for action. They say that by exploring the interconnectedness of language and emotions, we can reconstruct emotions in linguistic terms, and new options and opportunities appear that were previously transparent. If we examine the *actions* we are predisposed to perform when we experience a particular emotion, a further set of distinctions emerges that we can use to observe behavior. After observing a client's behavior and concomitant emotions, we can offer interventions that would otherwise not be available to us or the client. For example, when we are afraid, there is a whole range of actions we cannot take; when we feel secure, those actions are available to us. Further, if we consider the whole cluster of emotions included in fear as an emotion concerned with future loss, we can also assess that loss—its importance, its likelihood—and then investigate possible actions to prepare for it or prevent it. In the same way, if we look at sadness as an emotion concerned with past loss, we can assess that loss—its present importance and relevance—and investigate possible actions to let go of it. Anger reveals a fascinating mix of disparate emotions concerned with damage, which are often jumbled together and need to be separated to allow healing to begin. These emotions will be considered in more detail in Chapter 4.

Emotions, then, can be added to our palette of observations and can open a new range of possible actions and interactions. I am not claiming that emotions are linguistic, just that language not only provides a novel avenue for observing and naming emotions and preventing the inadvertent creation of unwanted, harmful emotions, but can also serve as an intervention by generating helpful, healing responses in our clients. Any additional way we can find of observing clients' experiences will contribute to the therapeutic benefits we have to offer them.

Moods and Emotions

Although moods and emotions are closely related, it is helpful to distinguish between them. In this context, an "emotion" is an experience triggered by a specific event, and a "mood" is experienced when no such event is relevant. Imagine a client who as a child was bitten by a dog and experienced an emotion of fear as a response to the event; now, when that client sees a dog or perhaps even thinks about a dog, the emotion of fear is triggered. The stimulus is the dog. When we are counseling clients, identifying the triggering event or situation can be helpful because the client can learn to avoid the situation or learn to have a different response to it:

A 10-year-old girl was brought to me by her mother because the girl had developed a phobia of spiders; she was having trouble going to sleep, then waking with nightmares about spiders. I asked her to bring me a project about spiders—a drawing she could make, some facts she could find, perhaps a story about spiders—and two weeks later she brought her project and proudly showed me. She told me about the number of legs and how they made their webs and showed me some cute drawings she had made. She then told me the story of Little Miss Muffett and laughed at Little Miss Muffett's silly behavior. She was not troubled with spider phobia after that.

In the past, when my children have wakened in the middle of a night terror because a monster is about to get them, they have all found it helpful to ask the monster what its name is. One even asked the monster if it would like a cup of tea. These conversations changed the emotion, and what had been problematic was now amusing.

Moods are different from emotions in important ways. A colleague described emotions as the surface turbulence of a river and moods as the deep currents. As distinct from emotions, moods don't have a triggering event but are experienced as an ambience, a background rumble, a general feeling. We have all awakened at times and felt wonderful or terrible "for no good reason." These are moods. Looking for a cause will be unhelpful because there isn't one. Finding some way to initiate some direct action, to help the client to do something different, will be pivotal.

Clinical depression is an example. Looking for causes for the mood of depression will only bring about frustration and possibly feelings of inadequacy when no cause can be found. The value of physical exercise in combating depression is well recognized and makes obvious sense within this understanding. Milton Erickson's directive "Whatever you do, get your client to *do* something" fits here precisely.

Humberto Maturana has described the interrelatedness of language and emotions as a braiding, which he calls "conversation." Conversation derives from the Latin *con* (meaning together) and *versare* (meaning to turn or change). How we speak and interact together affects how we feel and what we can do together. What we do together influences how we are able to speak with each other. This allows us to bring a particular mood to a counseling session—for example, a mood of caring, interest, and positive expectations—which can facilitate our clients being able to talk about what they need to. Our emotion generates the usefulness of the discussion. In addition, when we ask certain kinds of questions, such as "What's it like for you when the problem's not there or not so troublesome?" or "How will your experience be different when you've effectively dealt with the problem?" a certain kind of mood follows. In this case, we are generating a mood of optimism or hope which is always welcome when there are problems around.

THE EMBODIMENT OF EMOTIONS

As counselors, we are not used to dealing with physical symptoms or performing physical examinations of our clients' bodies. However, if we look at clients' body positions, their body language, their body movements, we can begin to observe *the body* as a whole and see something different, new, and useful in dealing with our clients' dilemmas. Looking at the body in this way opens a whole new world of observations, and the more observations we can make, the more useful we will be in helping clients find solutions.

We have lost contact with our body. Western culture ignores the body or punishes it, blames it, pushes it, starves it. Some religions consider it to be the home of the devil. Body workers unlock emotions, Feldenkrais practitioners free up the body, and dance therapists restore grace and presence to the body. But how can we reclaim our bodies and integrate them with our emotions so that we can be whole again and heal?

We can explore the connectedness between body posture and movements and emotions, generating new observations of ourselves, our past, and our future. By inventing a new arena for observing—in this case, the body—we open up another new world of distinctions that generates a whole new array of possibilities for our clients. We've already learned that problems are characterized by few options and are frequently solved by generating more options; therefore, it is relevant for us as therapists to generate as many options for clients as possible. In this way, we can further the effectiveness of what we have to offer clients:

A 33-year-old man reported that he had low self-esteem, which was making it difficult for him to socialize and meet women and was also interfering with his work performance. He had sought counseling several times previously and had gained some useful insights into why he was the way he was. He was a middle child, his elder sister had been chronically ill as a child, and his parents had separated when he was a teenager. These insights were interesting to him and had been of some assistance, but he was still concerned.

He was tall and thin, and walked with his shoulders down and forward. He tended to look at the ground in front of him, and there was little eye contact. He slumped in the chair and spoke softly and hesitantly.

Because he was a regular churchgoer, I asked him if he knew the 121st Psalm. Of course he did. "I will lift up mine eyes unto the hills, from whence cometh my help." He began to respond to the idea and raised his eyes, and his shoulders followed. I invited him to stand, planting his feet firmly and squarely on the floor, to bend his knees slightly so they weren't locked, and to straighten his shoulders. He stood tall, and when I asked him to gaze into the distance, just above the horizon, he was able to repeat the beginning of that psalm, and there was a wonderful shift in his mood. His face softened, his eyes opened and glistened, and there was a beginning of a smile. I then asked him to keep that position and speak out loud the words "I am who I am, and who I am is okay."

There was a dramatic transformation in this man as he said those words. The transformation was possible, not because of the words, but because he was able to create a body that could speak those words. Previously, they would have been mumbled and added to his dilemma.

He left with a new knowledge, a knowledge that was not intellectual but that gave him an experience that he could embody, that he could incorporate, own, and use. I invited him to practice this experience, telling him that like any new skill, some practice is often necessary.

By examining *the embodiment* of emotions or experiences, we generate the possibility of directly influencing the context or background of some aspect of the lives of our clients or ourselves. By shifting its ground, we may be able to transform it or learn how to enhance it. Our bodies can be thought of as the soil and our emotions the nutrients that allow our lives to grow. Enhancing the soil, adding vital nutrients, can transform the way growth proceeds.

We know that much of our learning has become automatic, and our body responds without the need for our awareness; certain tasks, places, and events trigger body reactions of pleasure or embarrassment even when we don't want them. All of these and a large range of other actions are experienced as if they are a direct expression of a body process.

We know from our everyday and professional experience that certain emotions are associated with certain body positions. In the same way that certain body positions can heighten the feeling of negative emotions, encouraging certain

A GUIDE TO OBSERVING EMOTIONS		
Emotion	**Where Emotion Is Experienced**	**How Emotion Is Experienced**
Anger		
A. Resentment	upper chest and throat	tight
	teeth and jaw	clenched
	eyebrows	down
	shoulders	pulled in
B. Frustration	forehead	tight
	stomach	tight
C. Indignation	whole body	upright, firm, strong
	breathing	deep
	heart	pounding
	stance	springy
	hands	"angry fist"
D. Rage	face	flushed
	arms	flailing
	eyes	blazing, unfocused
Fear		
A. Panic	heart	beating fast
	skin	sweaty
	breathing	shallow
	chest	tight
	stomach	nausea
	whole body	running paralyzed
B. Worry	hands	wringing
	lip, mouth	chewing
	teeth	clenched
	forehead	frown
C. Anxiety	stomach	knots
	breathing	quickens
	heart	palpitations
	palms	sweaty
	eyes	wide open
	whole body	fidgety
D. Anticipation	mouth	open
	eyes	shining
	whole body	pacing
E. Excitement	body	tingling
	heart	faster
	bladder and bowel	pressure
	mouth	smiling, laughing

60

Emotion	Where Emotion Is Experienced	How Emotion Is Experienced
Sadness		
A. Sad	chest	spacious
	shoulders	stooping
	eyes	crying
	head	fuzzy
B. Grief	whole body	heaving, empty, heavy, sobbing, convulsing, uncontrolled
	heart	aching, heavy
C. Despair	head	shaking, pounding
	body	sinking feeling, feeling detached, heavy
D. Anguish	whole body	silent scream, crushed, wrenched, rocking in fetal position
Positive Emotions		
A. Respect	body	still
	eyes	looking directly at object or person
	solar plexus	firm
	whole body	joining, blending, no boundaries
B. Humility	body	lowering, connecting, stillness
C. Fun	whole body	bouncing, laughing, singing
	face and eyes	smiling
D. Joy	chest	light, warm, open
	head	open

(Table title: A Guide to Observing Emotions (Continued))

positions can facilitate positive emotions in clients. For example, the body position we recognize as showing joy—open, receptive, soft face, hands, and torso—is not only an *expression* of the emotion of joy, but can also assist in *producing* the emotion. It is a two-way flow.

The table starting on page 60 contains a list of observations from various teaching and clinical situations. They are offered as a guide, as a set of distinctions, and can serve as a primer for those interested in making their own observations. These observations can be expected to vary widely from client to client and from observer to observer. Building a definitive list is less important than the process of looking, because it is by looking that we have the chance to see, by observing from a particular place (in this case, *the body*) that we have the opportunity to learn how to observe differently.

By observing the body in a variety of undesirable emotional states, we can speculate about what emotion the client may prefer; then, by shifting the body into that position, we can facilitate the emergence of that preferred emotion. This guide is offered, not as a substitute for the many effective approaches already used, but as an additional tool, for the more options we can offer our clients, the more useful we will be to them and the sooner they will be able to get on with their life.

CHAPTER Four

Emotional and Body Interventions

WE KNOW THAT OBSERVING body responses or "body language" is valuable. Because language is a two-way experience, we can invite clients to learn a new language for their body, a new body position and movements that will literally hold and support the changes that are desired. My Chilean colleague, Rafael Echeveria, said, "How we stand is how we stand in life, and how we move is how we move in life" (1994). It follows that if we can learn to stand and move differently, life will be experienced differently, and this can provide a whole new area of learning and experience for clients who are troubled and ask for our assistance.

Learning new body positions and movements can take time and experience. Providing an opportunity for clients to practice specific body positions and movements can make all the difference, more than merely observing what might need to be corrected. Exercise 1 (on pp. 66–67) is one to try yourself and to adapt to clients' individual requirements.

ANGER

Anger is an emotion familiar to all of us, and one that society has taught us to hide or control. But what is this powerful emotion about? Anger can take many forms. By lumping all forms of anger into the same category, we run the risk of gross inaccuracies. Let's closely examine four main types of anger: *resentment, indignation, frustration,* and *rage.*

Exercise 1: Observing the Body and Inviting Change

Ask a colleague or client to think of a problem in his or her life and use his or her body to express that problem:

❖ Notice the body position of the study partner or client.

❖ Place your own body in a similar position, and then ask yourself "What am I feeling?" You should experience a feeling or emotion that is easily recognized.

❖ Ask your partner or client "Are you feeling (insert what you are feeling)?"

This can add to your rapport with your study partner or client or to further exploration of what your partner or client is experiencing.

Next:

❖ Ask the colleague or client to change body position to how he or she would like to feel.

❖ Notice the new body position.

❖ Place your own body in a similar position, and then ask yourself "What am I feeling?" Again, it is expected that you will experience a feeling or emotion that you will easily recognize.

❖ Ask your partner or client "Are you now feeling (insert the feeling or emotion you are experiencing)?"

EXERCISE 1 *(Continued)*

❖ Ask your partner or client "Is this how you would prefer to feel?" If it is, consider asking your partner or client to stand and move about within that emotion, in that body position, and thereby learn or embody it.

This experience allows for a permanent shift in the client as a person, so that the new body experience, the preferred emotion, and the accompanying conversations and actions are a resource to be accessed in the future. Attending to this set of distinctions we are calling the body can have a useful impact on our clients and their possibilities in life.

Resentment

Resentment is created by a past experience of damage and a silent promise for revenge. Clients who are resentful may harbor a grumbling conversation in the background of their experience, recalling how a particular person did something harmful to them at some time in the past. They want revenge, compensation, blood.

Resentment is a pernicious emotion because it is double-edged: the resenter suffers at least as much as the resentee. If I am grumpy in the morning after my neighbors' rowdy party the night before, I am suffering from my grumpiness while they may be sleeping it off. Even worse, if resentment continues, it can get into our body and cause pain and illness: tension headaches, stress disorders, depression, even immune problems and malignancies. At the least, the resenter's life is placed on hold until the revenge or compensation is attained. We can be painfully aware of this dilemma in warring couples who ask for counseling and then begin to verbally demolish each other in our office.

Embodiment of Resentment

We can easily recognize the physical signs all too visible in the body of a resentful client: clenched jaw, red face, tight forehead and shoulders. The accompanying physical symptoms are also familiar: tension headaches, tension pains in the chest, dyspepsia, irritable bowel.

As well as attending to the life issues contributing to these problems, we can help clients deal with the problems more effectively. Sometimes resentment is the main cause of a continuing marital fight, and the conflict can subside as a result of dealing with the resentment directly. By working with the resentment, we can dissolve the problem. We can also assist clients to shift the resentment to a more useful emotion, such as indignation. Alternatively, we can set up an incongruity between the emotion and its embodiment, so that the problem situation disintegrates entirely:

A 45-year-old executive had been downsized and was angry at the way he had been informed. He had been losing sleep, was drinking too much, and was becoming irritable with his wife and children. When he spoke of his termination his jaw tightened, his eyes narrowed, and his whole body tensed. He hated the company, he hated the management style, he hated the person who had given him the news. I felt glad that I knew this man personally and was not his enemy. He recognized that his reaction was normal enough. He had observed a number of his colleagues go through similar experiences, and he wanted to move on, to put the pain and hurt behind him so he could get on with his life and begin to look for employment.

Because his jaw was painfully tense, I asked him to allow the muscles around his mandible to relax and to let his jaw begin to move from side to side. This loosening and novel movement produced a look of bemusement and the beginning of relief. I also asked him to soften the muscles around his eyes and play with how wide open they could be. I asked him to continue to move his jaw and eyelids in this manner and at the same time tell me how much he hated the company, the management, and so on. He began, but lost control, as the exercise seemed too funny to him. He laughed, rolled around in the chair, and after just a few minutes said he felt better, and he looked it. His face was relaxed, his eyes were warmer, his shoulders were looser. He was ready to go looking for a new job. I suggested that any time he felt the resentment returning, he knew what to do. He laughed some more.

EXERCISE 2: BREAKING UP EMBODIED RESENTMENT

❖ Clench your jaw and verbalize your resentment: "I resent . . ."

❖ Open your mouth, with a loose and floppy lower jaw.

❖ With your jaw floppy, repeat the verbalization of the resentment: "I resent . . ."

Clients often laugh as a result of the incongruence between the body and its emotion and the language; the resentment is then more difficult to reproduce.

Indignation

Indignation is a very different experience from resentment. Although both are responses to a past damage, the indignant response is a declaration that never again will we allow that person to damage us. Indignation is concerned with defending our personal space, our integrity, our dignity (hence "indignation"), and not surprisingly, it is a strengthening, "up" emotion that enlivens, invigorates, and motivates us to take better care of ourselves. I like indignation as an emotion and encourage it in my clients. In my view, if there were more indignation in the world, the world would be a more trustworthy place.

Embodiment of Indignation

Just as resentment is a contracting, gnawing, self-destructive emotion, indignation is an expanding, nourishing, self-enhancing emotion. A shift from resentment, with its secret promise for revenge on another person, to indignation, with its concern for personal dignity, is one of the most delightful human transformations to observe. It can look like the sun breaking through storm clouds as the body relaxes and straightens, the eyes clear, and the face softens. It can look like the person is returning to this world from the underworld and is more present, more available, more lively.

Many people have difficulty saying no, and the resulting resentment can adversely affect their health and well-being. How often do we hear, and even say, "I intended to say no, but when it came to the crunch, I weakened and said yes"? In these circumstances, it is as if the body can't let the word out. I have found it useful to ask clients who want to learn to say no to stand solidly in front of a mirror with their feet slightly apart, approximately shoulder-width, back straight,

---

EXERCISE 3: REPLACING
RESENTMENT WITH INDIGNATION

❖ Clench your jaw and say "I resent the damage you did to me in the past."

❖ Stand tall and straight with shoulders back and looking just higher than horizontal.

❖ Say in that position "I have been damaged in the past, but never again will I let you damage me in the future."

---

head high, and, looking their reflection in the eye, say no and notice how believable they are. The instant feedback can provide a delightful opportunity for the client to learn at the level of the body, not of the words, how to begin to have some effectiveness. By embodying the learning and practicing it as often as necessary, the client has a gentle and respectful experience to build on.

EXERCISE 4: BOOSTING SELF-CONFIDENCE

❖ Stand straight and tall, perhaps on a table or other elevated position.

❖ Look out into the distance.

❖ Say "I am who I am, and who I am is OK."

Frustration

Frustration is a held-in expressive or creative energy, like being "all dressed up with nowhere to go." We see this in our teenage children or clients when they are pacing the floor or when younger children are climbing up the walls. If we don't recognize their frustration and provide an acceptable outlet, we can also begin to climb the walls!

Embodiment of Frustration

When people are frustrated, their bodies can be either restless or looking as if they will burst with held-in energy. Relaxation or calming exercises may be relevant; alternatively, providing some creative outlet for expressing the frustration may defuse the emotion:

An executive was feeling overwhelmed by the challenging expansion of his business and was frustrated by his increasing paralysis in the face of the improvement in his career. He was agitated, restless, and becoming resentful. We went out into

---

EXERCISE 5: EXPRESSING FRUSTRATION

❖ Stomp about the room.

❖ Say "I'm so frustrated."

❖ Stand relaxed and comfortably still.

❖ Say "I can begin to (say something or take some action)."

the street, and I took his arm and walked with him at a very brisk pace. After only several minutes, he was unable to respond with frustration and could only feel bemused by his inactivity despite lots of work needing his attention. This brief walk of only several minutes shifted his mood sufficiently to allow him to make a start on the smallest and easiest of the steps his business required, and within a week he was back in the swing.

Rage

Rage is a form of anger in which we are taken over by some force that seems more powerful than we are; we feel compelled to carry out indiscriminate damage. In rage, we don't mind what or who we damage, including ourselves. Like Bluto in Popeye when he sees red, there is a kind of blindness to all but the compulsion of destruction.

Embodiment of Rage

The embodiment of rage, whether in someone else or in ourselves, is something we dread. The physical characteristics—red face, bloodshot eyes, tense facial muscles, clenched fists—along with the strength and unpredictability of movement are truly terrifying. We see it in wild animals and are justifiably in awe. Containment is the usual option, although the Zen invitation to control a wild bull by placing it in a large paddock may be a more human option if feasible.

Distinguishing these different forms of anger is not trivial. In a prison situation, for example, where rage needs to be contained for mutual safety, if frustration or resentment is handled by an attempt at containment, rage is likely to be generated. A riot can be produced in just this way.

Exercise 6: Preventing Rage

❖ Recognize *resentment* and shift it to acceptance or indignation.

❖ Provide opportunities for *frustration* to be expressed.

❖ Encourage the legitimacy of *indignation*.

Anger Summary

Recognizing types of anger can give us valuable clues to questions to ask in the counseling process. For example, when we recognize the anger as resentment, we can legitimately ask about damage in the past: "Did something happen to damage you?" We can examine the present importance of the damage: "That must have been terrible back then. Is it still affecting you now?" We can question the importance of vengeance: "Have you ever considered that you are continuing to suffer, while the person who damaged you back then is continuing to live his life?" We can bring up the possibility of accepting the damage, retiring the quest for vengeance, even forgiving.

When we recognize the anger as indignation, we can congratulate clients on their learning from their past damage and their determination to prevent a recurrence. We can ask how they might best take care of themselves in the future and encourage and support them in their determination to defend their dignity and personal integrity. Validating the legitimacy of clients' indignation can itself be reassuring.

When we recognize the anger as frustration, instead of trying to contain the emotion and potentially drastically worsening the situation, we can ask about what needs to be expressed, how this can best be achieved, what creative activities are already in place, what is the first and smallest step toward giving expression, and so forth. Again, assisting clients to recognize the legitimacy of their emotion can be what's needed.

By distinguishing among the different types of anger clients may be experiencing, we can assist them to shift their emotion to a more useful form. We saw that resentment is unhelpful, even harmful, and is a reaction to a past damage coupled with a promise for revenge. We also saw that indignation is a helpful, even healing emotion and is a reaction to a past damage coupled with a determination to prevent future damage. By making these observations, it then becomes possible to help clients to shift their resentment to indignation. This honors the validity of the past damage and permits clients to let go of their attachment to the suffering it caused and to transform that suffering into a strengthening of their personal integrity:

In a TV interview on ABC several years ago ("Did You Used to Be R.D. Laing?") R.D. Laing spoke of a woman who came to his Edinburgh psychiatric practice. She was in her late 20s. Her father had been having sex with her since she was a child, and this was continuing even though she was now married. She came for psychiatric treatment, but Laing had other, more down-to-earth, commonsense ideas. He suggested that she keep away from her father until she had learned to adequately defend herself. She took some lessons in self-defense, and when she was then able, she visited her father and told him that if he ever touched her again, she would kill him. She

presumably was able to speak so he could hear her and be-
lieve what she said because of the emotion in her speaking.

We can deduce from this account that the woman's emotion of helplessness, which is always accompanied by resentment, was transformed into indignation through her work with Laing. I was touched by Laing's account of this situation, and I continue to be inspired by it any time I recall it.

In his book, *Of Blood and Hope,* Samuel Pisar (1979) wrote of his liberation from Auschwitz at the end of World War II, of his experience of having to stop himself from resentfully perpetuating the atrocities he had witnessed as a prisoner when he felt like shooting an innocent German family. He also warned against forgetting the lessons of history lest they repeat themselves and invited us to keep the phrase "Never again" close at hand. This is a further example of the transformation of an embittered resentment into indignation and evokes the possibility of peace and cooperation on a larger scale:

Barbara is 54. She was raped by her father when she was 12, and the incest continued until she was 15. She has just found out that her younger sister was also raped. Neither Barbara nor her sister have ever discussed their experience before. Barbara's own marriage of 15 years is now looking very shaky. Her partner cannot deal with what she is telling him and Barbara feels he should be able to be more understanding. How would you approach this problem?

One of the most satisfying aspects of counseling is the experience of being a witness to someone's healing. It reminds me of my earlier experiences in obstetrics and the amazing appearance of a new life. So often, experiences like Barbara's are shrouded in shame and kept in place by the imperative of secrecy. The telling of the story can break the spell and allow the client to begin to thaw. Bill O'Hanlon describes such a problem as "frozen in time."

There are often very strong contradictory messages about incest—messages that cast doubt on clients' memory and experience. Clients sometimes doubt their own perception of reality and begin to split their experience; they think it happened, but at the same time, often they deny it. The issue of trust is thrown in everyone's face. How could someone who was supposed to love and protect the child be so hateful, abusive, and uncaring?

Listening respectfully and supportively can be the cure. Asking questions such as "What have you already done to resolve this for yourself?" and "What else might you need to do to let go of your suffering about this terrible experience?" can also be helpful. Offering a respectful presence to validate the client's telling of the story can be a moving experience, and having evidence from another (in Barbara's case, her sister) helps to resolve some of the self-doubt that otherwise can be detrimental to healing.

The second issue in this scenario is Barbara's shaky marriage. Acknowledging the difficulty of not being supported by her partner of 15 years and attempting to release Barbara from resenting that lack of support can lead to healing. Reminding Barbara that her partner may not have the capacity to support her in the way she wants can help to normalize the situation. Releasing her from the vain attempt to get something that doesn't seem to be there might focus her energies on what she can do to resolve her problem.

Barbara is likely to feel massive resentment toward her father, and she will need to find some way of expressing that that will bring healing for her. Writing a letter that she doesn't send or having an imagined conversation with him in which she can express her grievances can help bring resolution. In my experience, the most important emotion to express here is indignation. Asking Barbara to stand up, strong and firm, and say out loud, as if talking to her father, something like "I want you to know that what you did to me really hurt me and damaged me, and I am never ever going to let you hurt me or damage me in the future" can allow Barbara to experience a sense of self-control and power she may not have felt before.

It is a beautiful experience to watch strength return to a client, bringing with it a sense of being back in the driver's seat of his or her life. When this happens, there is no turning back, no retreating into the previous role. It reminds us of why we are doing the kind of work we are.

SADNESS

Sadness is an emotion we experience when we find ourselves dealing with a past loss. When there has been a loss of some importance—a loved one, a work position, an ability, some aspect of our identity—we are predisposed to feel some sort of sadness. Because some losses are more strongly felt, more important, and of greater significance, we experience different responses. The loss of a shopping list is experienced differently from the loss of a family member. The degree of importance that we attribute to what has been lost determines our response.

Many other factors have an effect here, as well. How many times have we heard a client say "I know my husband has died, but I just can't accept it"? How is it that we humans can say in the same breath that we acknowledge that something has happened, yet we cannot accept that it has happened? It sounds insane, yet it is very normal.

We also have a very different response to loss according to how we assess our ability to manage the consequences of the loss. Some entrepreneurs who go bankrupt can take a deep breath and launch themselves into the next multimillion-dollar venture. They have ridden the wave and crashed before, they will again, so they can handle it. At other times, we might miss a train or have someone put a minor dent in our car at the supermarket parking lot, and we are barely able to contain ourselves. We can feel desperate, ready to kill ourselves or someone else, yet it is just a dent.

When we examine some of these responses, we can begin to identify some useful patterns that will help us focus in dealing with our own and our clients' emotional responses to loss. Depending on whether we can accept the loss or not, whether we assess that we can handle the loss ourselves or not, whether we accept the possibility of outside help arriving or not, we can find ourselves in a wide range of emotions in the general area of sadness.

Sadness

We can distinguish sadness as an emotion in which we are predisposed to *accept* a loss. We can observe this phenomenon if we look carefully with our clients. Clients may be discussing their suffering over the loss of a spouse, a pet, a position, or whatever, and as the counseling session progresses, they can show a subtle but pivotal change in their emotional state. As they speak, the pain subsides, the suffering abates, the tightness in their voice dissolves, and a calmness arrives, a look of peace, of something resolving. The clients are accepting the loss as a loss. Their eyes fill and overflow with tears, not of pain but of relief. This is the sign of acceptance leading to resolution and peace. This is the beauty of sadness.

We have misunderstood sadness as an undesirable emotion. We feel compelled to help someone "cheer up." When we recognize sadness as a sign of acceptance, we can encourage the expression of the sadness, reassuring clients that the sadness they are experiencing is the healing, the desired and healthy emotion. This can circumvent clients feeling a healthy sadness and then generating conflict about the sadness, avoiding it and so prolonging their suffering. I have developed a profound appreciation for sadness and claim that if there were more sadness in the world, there would be less suffering and more peace.

The Embodiment of Sadness

I have found that encouraging the bodily expression of sadness by crying is one of the most useful and resolving experiences I can offer as a therapist. We have all felt better after a good cry. There is something deeply healing about letting go of the impossible hope that someone or something we know is gone forever will return, and reconnecting with the reality of the loss. By letting go of the impossible hope, we can then get on with the reality of our life and build a future.

EXERCISE 7: ACCEPTING SADNESS

❖ Sadness can be accepted and encouraged as a normal part of coming to terms with a loss.

❖ Think of a loss which is irretrievable.

❖ Acknowledge the importance of who or what was lost.

❖ Examine any possible ways of retrieving the loss.

❖ If there are none, begin to sit with this experience.

❖ Notice your experience.

This runs contrary to the popular idea that when people are sad, they need to cheer up or simply get on with their life. My experience is that after sadness has been fully experienced (and this experience will be vastly different for different individuals), then and only then does cheerfulness appear spontaneously and the client is ready to move on.

Grief

We can distinguish grief as an emotion in which we are predisposed to *not yet accept* a loss that we know to be a loss and so suffer terribly in the process. Knowing that something has happened and refusing to acknowledge that it has is a recipe for suffering. The conflict that results from knowing that something is so, and yet not accepting that it is so, is agonizing.

If we can recognize a client in grief, we can ask about the loss, confident that there will have been a loss of importance. We can affirm the importance of that loss and legitimize the degree of suffering. We can inquire about what the client has already done to begin to accept the loss, to begin to come to terms with the reality of the loss, what has already happened that has been helpful. We can ask clients how they will know when the acceptance has happened, what others will notice that would let them know that they are beginning to accept the loss, that they are getting ready to continue on with their life with adequate respect for the loss.

This observation, coupled with these kinds of questions, can assist clients to move through their time of grief, to process their grief, to resolve it, and to move toward acceptance. It can be helpful to look for the tell-tale signs of sadness and acknowledge those signs with clients. By noticing their peaceful tears or a change in their facial expression toward calmness and acceptance, we can help to consolidate those changes and make them last.

The Embodiment of Grief

Grieving is a natural, normal process when there has been a loss. How can we assist someone to make the journey? Some are reluctant to begin, fearful of being overwhelmed or drowned by the experience; others seem to be stuck in the pain of grieving and don't know how to complete the journey. Clients may consult us to have our permission or support so they can feel safe to begin the journey or to have permission or help completing it. We can help by saying "It's OK to feel the pain" or asking "How near are you to accepting the loss?" or "What else might you do to help let the loss rest?" or even "How will you know when you have grieved sufficiently?"

Because grief indicates that one hasn't fully accepted the loss, the resulting conflict seems to beg for resolution. We can assist clients to move toward acceptance in our conversations about acceptance, and we can also help by changing their body posture. We can encourage clients to relax any tightness in their shoulders, to loosen and open their hands, to lift their gaze, straighten their spine, and let the muscles of their face soften, particularly their forehead and around their eyes. We can ask them to sit comfortably, perhaps with their head bowed forward, eyes downcast, and ask how they feel about their loss. The bending forward of the head can facilitate the experience and the expression of sadness. We can ask clients to place their hands on their lap, with their palms turned upward as an expression of acceptance, of receiving. We can speak in a kindly tone, expressing our acceptance of their suffering, and because moods are infectious, clients can begin to feel acceptance themselves:

A woman in her late 20s said that she hadn't gotten over the death of her father some 10 years previously. She hadn't gone to the funeral (in her family, women don't go to funerals), and he wasn't spoken about in family conversations. Her mood was flat, and there was no joy in her life. She said she felt numb, as if her feelings were on hold. I asked her to visit her father's grave and imagine that she could speak with him. After I reassured her that this really was an acceptable thing to do, she agreed.

Afterward, she told me that she had a lot to say to him. After she got past her embarrassment, she told him how much she missed him, how important he had been to her. Then she was surprised to find herself feeling angry, even telling him that she was annoyed that he had left her without the support she wanted and expected from him as a father. After saying all this, she was overcome with a strong sense of emptiness and then sadness as she came to accept that although she was speaking, there was no one responding. The reality sank in. She went home and had a long sleep, waking up the next morning feeling relieved and free. She began to notice the garden outside the window and reported to me that she was thinking of going out dancing.

Exercise 8: Resolving Grief

❖ Acknowledge the importance of the loss.

❖ Normalize the experience as leading to acceptance.

❖ Ask "How long do you anticipate needing to arrive at acceptance?"

❖ Ask "What is an appropriate amount of time to take, given the nature of your loss?"

❖ Ask "What has been helpful to get you this far?"

Anguish

We can distinguish anguish as an emotion in which we are predisposed to look beyond ourselves for help because our problem seems overwhelming. Anguish is the emotion of acute loss: we lose someone or something of great importance to us and are totally overwhelmed. The loss seems far beyond our capacity to deal with it, and yet the suffering is of such intensity that we feel compelled to do something. It is this pull between a compelling need to act and feeling that the action needed is beyond us that makes this emotion so agonizingly painful. We feel torn apart, ripped open, undone.

As counselors, we can provide the support, reassurance, and comfort that is demanded by clients dealing with anguish. When we recognize anguish, we can normalize the emotion: "After such a loss, who wouldn't be devastated" or "Given the importance of (the loss) to you, it's no wonder that you are feeling this way" or "You are having a normal, healthy reaction to a situation that would overwhelm any healthy person." These kinds of responses can allow the process of settling, of acceptance to begin. By first legitimizing the anguish, we can help the client avoid becoming stuck in the pain; then the client can surrender to it as a part of the healing.

The Embodiment of Anguish

Picasso's *Face of a Crying Woman* expresses the face of anguish. We feel despair that the problem is beyond our capacity to cope and also physical pain from not recognizing the possibility of any help in any form appearing from any source. Anguish has been described as the dark night of the soul, a place that most of us have visited and to which we don't want to return.

One difficulty therapists need to take care of here is our own mood. If a client is suffering from anguish and can't see a way to let go of it at the time, unless we recognize their right as a free citizen of a free society to suffer until they choose not to, we can find ourselves beginning to suffer with them. This is of no help to anyone, including our clients. Seeing that we are suffering because of their suffering can escalate the situation, and so it is preferable for us to be accepting of their suffering, their right to suffer, and to let them know that we can cope:

A man in his late 30s had recently separated from his second wife after a two-year attempt to make the marriage work. He said the situation was particularly bad because she had run off with another woman and taken all the family photos and keepsakes and most of the furniture. He was in debt, was feeling desperately lonely, and couldn't get a grip on anything. He vacillated between grieving for the loss of his marriage, resentment that she had left, and despair that there didn't seem to be anything he could do to help himself. He had previously been a self-reliant, macho type who prided himself on his physical strength and endurance.

I asked him if there was any chance of his wife's returning. After contemplating the question, he responded that even though he missed her terribly, there was no way that he would have her back again. I asked him to notice what he had just said, and he began to let his own words percolate into his experience so he could hear them. He began to weep, something that he had been doing increasingly and was acutely embarrassed by. I suggested that he continue to let the tears flow, as they were his body's sign of acceptance that his marriage was over. He then began to sob, and his physical pain was palpable. I sat with him, reassuring him that he was OK, that it was OK to be upset, even helpful to be upset, and that I was willing to do whatever I could to help him. After 10 minutes or so, he began to settle. He was slumped forward, looking in the direction of his heavy boots.

EXERCISE 9: RESOLVING ANGUISH

❖ Normalize anguish as a normal reaction to an overwhelming situation.

❖ Legitimize the need for outside help.

❖ Ask "What kind of help has been useful in the past?"

❖ Ask "Who could give such help now?"

---

*He said that he was beginning to accept the fact that there
was no going back, and I encouraged him to continue with
that acceptance. Some minutes later, I asked him to stand up,
put his shoulders back, look out the window at the sky and
the clouds, and notice what he was beginning to discover. He
said, "There is a light at the end of the tunnel," and when I
quipped "Are you sure it's not an oncoming train, or hasn't
just been turned out due to an industrial dispute?" he actually smiled.*

Despair

Despair is an emotion in which we find ourselves resigned
to the absence of possibility of outside help, even though
we know it is the only thing that will save the day. Someone
said that despair is like being surrounded by enemies, hoping that the cavalry will come and save us, yet realizing that
the cavalry aren't coming!

Because an integral component of despair is an element
of resignation, this must be addressed before any healing
can happen. Our first step is to begin to reawaken the
client to the possibility that despair will pass. Resignation

is a mood in which we are blind to possibilities for change, and within resignation, possibilities show up as vain hopes. We can comfort our clients and reassure them of our support. When we sit with them through their despair, they can begin to recognize that time is passing and they are surviving, and maybe, just maybe, there is a light at the end of the tunnel.

Our willingness to sit with and be with the client in this way is in itself healing. It requires that we be willing to sit with our own experience of helplessness and actively refrain from interfering, as that would only diminish the experience for the client and prolong the suffering.

With time and support, despair can transform into anguish, possibly then into grieving, and finally to the beautiful, light emotion of peaceful acceptance. It is one of the privileges of our work that we can witness this process. Just as we see the body heal with support and appropriate help, we can see the emotions heal and clients become whole persons again, realistically knowing that they have experienced a loss and then experiencing the peace that acceptance fosters.

The Embodiment of Despair

In a laboratory experiment, rats were placed on a metal plate that was electrified intermittently. Before long the rats didn't even move, although they looked as if they were experiencing pain. There was nowhere to go, there was nothing they could do, so they stopped trying to escape. Despair is a terrible emotion, dehumanizing and soul damaging. We see it in the faces of victims of war and crime. We want to turn away, and yet the emotion is so strong there is a compulsion to continue watching.

Dealing with despair is particularly difficult in our Western society with our emphasis on individuality and self-reliance. We should be able to handle this ourselves, we shouldn't ask for help, and yet to be experiencing despair means that we are out of our depth, and outside help is necessary.

I like to recite the words of the psalmist: "I will lift up mine eyes unto the hills, from whence cometh my help." To walk in the wild and look up at the treetops, the sky, and the clouds allows us to reconnect with the larger world we live in, a perspective we often easily miss. When we work with clients experiencing despair, asking them to stand firm, lift their shoulders and hold them back, and lift their gaze to a point just above an imagined horizon can bring about a refreshing change in their outlook. From this position, all kinds of help and support appear for the first time. If we look at our feet, that's what we see; if we look up and out, our perspective broadens. How and where we look gives us access to different worlds of experience.

EXERCISE 10: RESOLVING DESPAIR

❖ Encourage clients to experiment with new body positions that might make their despair seem less threatening and allow new possibilities to emerge.

❖ Take the client for a walk during therapy rather than sit in your office. Help the client to notice the surroundings and experience what is going on outside the self, allowing the client to shift from an internalizing to an externalizing perspective.

❖ Find out who might be able to make emotional contact with this client and encourage the client to spend time with that individual.

FEAR, GUILT, AND SHAME

Fear

We have seen that the emotion of anger is concerned with damage and that sadness is an emotion concerned with past loss. We can then observe and distinguish the different kinds of damage or loss and the responses to that damage or loss and give clearer guidance to our clients to assist their learning and healing.

Fear is a collection of predispositions to act in relation to a future loss. If we anticipate that we may lose someone or something in the future, we feel some form of fear. The kind of fear we experience depends on the degree of importance we place on the loss, and also on the influence of time. We can distinguish *worry, anxiety,* and *panic* as types of fear and further identify two related emotions: *anticipation* and *excitement.*

Because every client is unique, it is always important to remind ourselves that we are never dealing with a condition, a syndrome, or even an emotion, but always with an individual. If we forget this, we can make assumptions that will interfere with the effectiveness of the counseling process. When clients say "I'm anxious," "I'm frightened," or "I'm panicking," we have a good idea about their experience from working with others or from our own experience. But, although experience can be helpful in making general sense of the situation, it brings the risk of missing what this particular client is experiencing and what this particular client needs to deal with his or her situation.

One way of clarifying the situation is to put what we know in the background, put it on hold for the moment, and ask clients how they are experiencing their situation. For example, we could say, "When you say you are anxious, I am sure you know what that means to you, but so I can best help you, it would be useful if you could explain to me just how the anxiety you are experiencing is affecting you in specific ways." Asking such a question can clarify the situation for us and sometimes for the client as well. It can alert us to the degree of importance placed on the anticipated loss, as well as its immediacy. Both factors are relevant to offering help that is fitting.

It can also be useful to ask clients what is missing, what would alleviate their anxiety, panic, worry, or fear. In anxiety, calmness or a sense of security may be missing; in panic, it may be time, a way to slow down, or a way to alleviate pressure. If we don't ask, we are left with our best guess, and that will be just that—a guess.

Worry

Worry is an emotion in which we find ourselves concerned with a loss of variable importance at some time in the future, ranging up to decades. We can worry about who will come to our funeral, even if we are not anticipating dying for another 50 years. We can worry about how we will cope with changes, even if we don't have any idea about what those changes might be. The important factor here is to recognize that there is no need to act in the immediate future; we can act at some future time. This can be helpful in conversing with worried clients as we can legitimize their concern about the future loss and then ask when they should begin to actually do something about it. Providing an opportunity to reflect on the time factor can be liberating. Clients may decide that no action is required now, or they can begin to make some small preparations and move into action. In either situation, the worry is dealt with.

EXERCISE 11: LIFTING WORRY

❖ Frown, slump your shoulders forward, and look down at the ground.

❖ Say "I'm worried about a lot of things."

❖ Straighten your body, look at the horizon.

❖ Say "Circumstances may improve or worsen, but I have time to consider all my options."

Embodiment of Worry.   In a mood or emotion of worry, we readily recognize the furrowed brow, partly closed eyes, stooped shoulders, and downcast gaze.

Anxiety

We can observe anxiety in clients when they experience a concern for a future loss requiring action in the near future—perhaps the next few months, weeks, or days. The observation of time here guides us in our conversations with anxious clients so that we can validate their concern about losing whatever it is that is important to them and help them to discover what time is available, what actions need to be taken, when to prepare for the loss, and perhaps how to prevent it. In the emotion of anxiety, we don't have the luxury of more or less unlimited time; we need to get started fairly soon.

Embodiment of Anxiety.   In anxiety, the body is more alert: eyes open, looking randomly about, with agitated movements of the arms, wringing of hands, and restlessness of the feet.

EXERCISE 12: SOFTENING ANXIETY

❖ Get your body ready for some unknown action.

❖ Say "I have to do something soon, but I won't be able to cope."

❖ Shift your body to a settled, still position, eyes resting on some pleasant object.

❖ Say "Whatever happens, I will find a way of coping."

Panic

In the emotion of panic, the future loss is experienced as imminent. In panic, we feel compelled to act *now*. A delay of even a few minutes may be too much. Panic is the emotion of emergency situations where seconds count. In the presence of a house fire or other life-threatening event, action needs to be immediate. In a dysfunctional situation, clients may feel as if their life is in danger in the face of no evidence; they panic about "nothing." We say it's nothing, but to a panicking person, even though there is obviously plenty of air in a plane, as the plane door is closed, that person can feel in danger of suffocation and feel compelled to get out. When they see a spider in the car, clients with a spider phobia might attempt to get out even while the car is moving at high speeds; the emotion of panic circumvents the usual process of assessing the risks of staying in the car with the spider or getting out. The client feels compelled to act immediately.

When clients are panicking, we must reassure them and even physically restrain them if necessary to protect them. We intuitively know from our past experience that panic requires immediate help. It follows that a client who suffers panic attacks will require some method of containing the experience that acts immediately, not in an hour's time.

Embodiment of Panic. When we observe panicking clients' body position—often tight and drawn in with legs clamped together, wringing hands, wide-eyed—or their body movement—often stiff and quick little movements of hands and eyes—we must consider what body position and body movement may be more helpful.

The first step is to help clients relax. Help them to discover how it feels to sit back in a chair and begin to let their limbs rest for a time, let their eyes close comfortably. It may be helpful to alert their attention to the security of the floor under their feet, the chair supporting their back, the way the walls and ceiling of the room are OK. It may also be helpful to invite them to stand with their legs securely on the floor in line with their shoulders, with their shoulders held back and head erect, and to look at some point just above the level of an imagined horizon. They could begin to observe how pleasing it is to notice the regular and peaceful way they can breathe in and out, becoming aware of the difference in the air as it is breathed in from how it feels as it is breathed out. They could then be invited to begin to swing their upper body or rotate it so that one then the other shoulder rotates forward. By shifting body position or body movement, the more desired emotional state is accessed and clients are then more able to feel the way they want to feel:

A woman in her 50s disentangled herself from a destructive marriage of 30 years and was left with a severe anxiety about heights. This was coming to a head, as she had to go to court for the divorce and the court was on the tenth floor! I drove her to the building where the court was and asked her to stomp on the footpath outside and notice how solid it was. She en-joyed the experience. We then went into the foyer and again I asked her to test the solidness of the floor. When she was well satisfied with the construction, I informed her that there were several floors of underground parking under her feet and in-vited her to recognize how unimportant that was. When I re-minded her that on the ground floor she was already some distance up, yet the floor felt just fine under her feet, she was able to experience the solidness of the elevator, and also the floor outside the elevator on the tenth floor. The floor was va-cant, and it was difficult for me to restrain her childlike en-thusiasm after she had tested the solidness of the floor in various empty offices and then pressed her face against the windows, looking at the cars and people below, excited at how small they all looked. She was able to go to the court, complete the divorce proceedings, and continue to enjoy elevators and other experiences involving heights.

EXERCISE 13: DIFFUSING PANIC

❖ Ask clients to notice their feet.

❖ Ask them to notice the solidness of the ground or floor.

❖ Ask them to breathe slowly and easily.

❖ Walk with them—with slow and firm steps.

❖ Draw their attention to the first signs of the panic's subsiding.

Anticipation and Excitement

We recognize these emotions in our own experience when we look forward with pleasure to some future event. The concern with loss here is the fear that the event may *not* happen. Children's excitement at their upcoming birthday party includes concern that there won't be any presents, or not the presents they wanted. Some of us get excited on a roller-coaster ride because the fear of damaging ourselves is contained, and we can anticipate surviving the experience; it is the small risk of not surviving, however, that gives the edge to the experience.

Embodiment of Anticipation and Excitement. A person experiencing anticipation or excitement about an upcoming event may embody this emotion by becoming agitated and restless but at the same time show signs of enjoyment. There may be fleeting doubts showing on the face like clouds across the sun, reflecting concern about the desired outcome not happening. But the sun comes out again.

Guilt and Shame

When we experience guilt, there is always a damaging of some personal standard, whereas shame is experienced when some social standard is broken. These two emotions often go together, but it is essential that we distinguish them if we are to help clients overcome them.

Guilt

When clients complain of feeling guilty, we can ask them what personal standard has been brought into question. This is affirming to clients and at the same time offers us an opportunity to comment about their high personal standards. When we validate their experience, they are then in a better position to deal with the problem; when we reframe the situation in this way, clients may even be able to dissolve the problem. When someone complaining of feeling guilty is complimented on his or her high moral standards, that person is then bound to acknowledge his or her personal worth or give up the guilt. High standards are a prerequisite for guilt; psychopaths, having no personal conscience, are not capable of feeling guilt. This affirming, validating conversation can be sufficient to dissolve the guilt in some situations. If it isn't, we can ask "How much longer will you need to suffer the guilt to wipe the slate clean, or to have served your time?" This can bring the situation back to earth and reconnect clients with the reality of life and assist them to deal with the conflict by resolving it at the same level at which the problem was generated:

A successful entrepreneur was having difficulty signing his name at work. He felt that, as it was his business, he should

---

EXERCISE 14: RESOLVING GUILT

❖ Acknowledge the guilt and legitimize it.

❖ Compliment clients on having high moral standards (i.e., reframe).

❖ Ask about what moral standard in particular is being challenged.

❖ Offer the possibility that they may have suffered enough already to compensate for the guilt—they may have served their time.

---

be able to manage this easily, just as he was able to maintain the high standards of his management team. I asked him one of my favorite riddles, which I adapted from Milton Erickson: "If you and Superman had a race to the equator, who would get there first?" To which he replied, "Superman, of course!" I informed him that because I was asking the question, it was up to me to know the right answer, and his answer was wrong. When he asked why he was wrong, I had pleasure in telling him "You would get there first—because there ain't no such person as Superman." He got the message about his high personal standards and was able to relax enough to easily get past his signing difficulty.

Shame

Shame is different from guilt. Because shame is an emotion in which some social standard has been transgressed, there is nothing that can be done effectively on a personal level. To deal with shame, we need some social experience. Again, it can help to recognize and affirm that the presence of a social standard requires a particular kind of individual—one who is socially responsible—and simply breaking the silence that shame insists on can assist clients. But often, some public event is required to fully deal with shame.

For example, gay men and women can overcome any guilt about their sexual preference by resolving their personal experience, but it is only by "coming out" to a gay community or to the wider community that any shame is dissolved. The same process applies to many of life's experiences, both positive and negative. It's not "cool" for teenagers to admit that they like schoolwork or that they love their parents, and saying it to their friends or family can free them from the shame they might otherwise feel:

A woman in her mid-40s wanted help with her problem getting back to work after multiple position changes and eventually a demotion. While off work, coming to terms with her situation, she had the additional problem of discovering that a breast lump was malignant and had surgery. She was guilty about not being able to cope with the changes at work and felt shame about her mastectomy. Part of her counseling process was to come to terms with her human limitations, allowing her guilt to subside. But the shame had led to her keeping her physical problem secret from her friends, leading to increasing isolation.

When I asked her who would be the easiest person to tell about her operation, she decided that person would be a close friend she had since school. After telling this friend what had happened, she was then able to tell enough of her other close friends to dispel her shame, and her healing—emotional and social—could progress.

Embodiment of Shame.   Shame requires secrecy to be maintained, so the body is contracted as if trying to become invisible: head down, gaze furtive, shoulders stooped.

EXERCISE 15: RELIEVING SHAME

❖ Straighten your body and lift your head.

❖ Think of a person with whom you can share your secret.

❖ How will you feel when you have broken the spell and spoken about this?

❖ Who else will notice the changes?

CREATING EMOTIONAL HEALTH

We can observe repeatedly that the language we use influences the outcome of our work with clients, and even their future health. Asking clients how they are doing, asking about their problem, or asking about improvements in their situation creates different outcomes that are not just semantic. We've noted how helpful it can be to ask clients what pleases them in their life, what they enjoy. Asking these questions helps to restore the balance of their experience and correct the imbalance that problems always bring.

Alerting clients to times when the problem is less troublesome or perhaps not there at all is an invitation for them to attend to the experience of problem-free times and so learn from their own experience about how to have more of those times. It can be helpful to clients, and satisfying to us, to ask them to look for improvements between sessions. This can help shift their orientation away from the problem; viewing the experience in a new light, clients actually have a different experience—one that is more desirable.

We can also observe that moods and emotions have a very powerful influence on experience, ours and our clients', an influence that had been transparent to us earlier. We intuitively know about moods and emotional responses, but until recently we have not made the fullest use of our knowledge. For example, if we recognize the various faces of anger as being concerned with damage, we can examine with the client the reality of the perceived damage, its present relevance, and what can be done to take care of the situation. If we can observe sadness as concerned with past loss and look to see what degree of acceptance has been reached, we might be able to facilitate further movement toward acceptance and peace. Recognizing fear as an emotion concerned with future loss alerts us to inquire about the importance of the loss, its impact, and what can be done to prepare for or prevent it.

There has been a change of emphasis in mental health practice from being concerned solely with diagnosis, treatment, and curing illness to including illness prevention and, more recently, health promotion. We read about health being more than an absence of disease, that health is a condition we, as counselors, can help to generate. Knowing that language is generative and that emotions provide the soil for growing different experiences, we need to ask ourselves what kinds of language, what kinds of emotions, and what kinds of changes in body posture and movement are going to help the germination and strong development of health.

In response to these questions, the language forms addressed in this book take on additional importance. Asking about clients' likes, their problem-free experiences, and improvements they have already noticed is going to have an active influence on their general mood and sense of well-being.

There are some folks who bemoan the fact that nothing seems to go right in their life, and they can usually provide ample evidence for this. Similarly, people who report that they live a charmed life can also produce at least as much evidence. It is as if our emotions are a force field that attracts certain activities and opportunities and repels others. We all know, with or without evidence, that when we feel good, life generally goes better, but we often talk about our emotions as if they were some kind of internal weather—difficult to predict, unreliable, and able to change at any moment for no apparent reason. By fostering positive emotions we can keep clients' lives on a more even keel. We can do this through our conversations with clients but also by encouraging positive body postures and movements.

There is a collection of positive emotions that are familiar enough to us, yet we often experience a shortage of them.

These include gratitude, joy, pride, fun, celebration, intimacy, wonderment, love, peace, and acceptance. These emotions can be transparent to us: when we are happy, we (and our clients) hardly notice it. It's only when the happiness passes that we experience something vague, like something not there, although it would be difficult to specify the experience exactly. We also tend to think that we are passive participants in these emotions, even when we do distinguish them. We also know that simply telling a client, or ourselves, to "cheer up and be happy" is not a reliable way of generating happiness.

At the same time, we have some sense that we are not entirely helpless here. We know intuitively that there are some activities or interactions that foster certain emotions in us. There are particular people whom we like to be with because we are more content or playful or peaceful around them. We often choose our friends this way, as people whom we like to visit and hang out with. It's not so much what we do together but rather the way we can be together, perhaps sharing their mood, or their sharing our mood, or both sharing a mood generated by the interaction:

A woman in her 50s complained of feeling empty and worthless and of having almost constant headaches in her temples and around her eyes. Tests and specialist opinions were normal. She said she had worked all her life but had recently become unemployed. In addition, her mother had recently died, and her grandchildren were estranged after her son's remarriage. When I asked her how she would rather feel, she was excited to tell me that she would rather feel useful. She missed the interaction with children most of all. She made inquiries about part-time cleaning to supplement her pension, and visited children in hospital for two half-days a week.

She knew the emotion she wanted and needed very little help to have it again, once both of us were able to identify the missing emotion of usefulness and look to find ways of encouraging it. The headaches subsided spontaneously and she began to visit other members of her family more frequently.

Respect

Respect is a delightful emotion. Respect "blesses he that gives and he that takes": by respecting another person or creature, we are granting legitimacy to that other to exist, to be just so, and at the same time, we are influenced personally, feeling humble, connected, grounded. Respect reconnects us to the experience of who we are, and at the same time reconnects us to a larger experience—something beyond our individual person.

Embodiment of Respect

One of my Chilean teachers, Julio Olalla, helped me to recognize that I didn't need to belittle others who were more skilled than I to be comfortable with them. He taught me that I can accept that I have more skills in some areas of life, and others have more skills in other areas. I could acknowledge

---

EXERCISE 16: PROMOTING RESPECT

❖ Place your body in an open position: face relaxed, hands open, shoulders relaxed.

❖ Think of someone who has shared concerns.

❖ Acknowledge the commonality.

❖ Silently give the other permission to be how he or she is.

my competencies and theirs without the need for competition or even comparison. When I heard that and saw how obvious and useful that was, I noticed that my face softened, my shoulders dropped, my stomach relaxed, and my mood changed from one based in fear to one based on acceptance. This was an experience of respect. Now, when I start to feel competitive or defensive or insecure toward another person, I intentionally relax my stomach, loosen my shoulders, and soften the muscles of my face, which allows the experience of respect to appear.

Gratitude

Gratitude is an emotion in which we are predisposed to be thankful. America as "the Land of Plenty," Australia as "the Lucky Country," and the United Kingdom as "the Welfare State" have influenced our Western culture to expect rights and privileges as given and not needing to be worked for, earned, or deserved. This tendency to take what we have for granted is something I observe in our children as rampant generally in our society. I feel some sadness when there is no appreciation of what we have or what we are given. The boredom and disgruntledness that is spreading is directly related to a lack of gratitude, in my observation. "Thank you" is an expression that could be listed as endangered and worth preserving before it becomes extinct. We can foster gratitude by practicing thankfulness:

A woman in her 60s complained of feeling burdened by the worries of her physical aging and associated family pressures. Her husband was a considerate man, understanding by nature, but had his own pressures to cope with. He asked her what she was writing in a diary, and she informed him that it was a "gratitude journal" in which she was recording five things each day she could be grateful for. She explained that sometimes the quota was filled in unexpected ways. Simply noting down some everyday happenings such as drinking a cup of tea or reading a magazine made them more notice-able, and her appreciation of these experiences spilled over into her conversations with her husband and her daughter.

Embodiment of Gratitude

Gratitude allows us to feel appreciation for a gift, connects us with the giver, and humbles us in the larger picture of a wide and diverse world. The Australian novel *A Fortunate Life* by A. B. Facey (1981) reminds us that gratitude can shape our experience and allow us to appreciate what we do have and what we can do, and frees us from the constraints of resentment for what we don't have and can't do. Anyone reading about Facey's life might think it was anything but fortunate, but for him, it was.

EXERCISE 17: PROMOTING GRATITUDE

- ❖ Sit quietly, hands on thighs, palms uppermost.
- ❖ Soften your facial muscles, particularly around your eyes.
- ❖ Think of who is important in your life.
- ❖ Imagine thanking them.
- ❖ Think of possessions you have that are precious.
- ❖ Imagine thanking someone for them.
- ❖ Notice your experience, and memorize it.

The body responds to this emotion by softening and becoming energized. There is often a widening of the eyes, a lifting of the head, a straightening of the spine, and a pulling back of the shoulders. This observation provides the marvelous opportunity to intentionally put our body in such a position and so naturally enhance the experience of gratitude.

Joy

Joy is an emotion in which we are grateful to life for no good reason—when we are grateful to life itself for our very existence. There are many social rituals that can generate thankfulness to life. For example, most major religions contain opportunities to give thanks for our birth, our family, our food, and so on. But we often forget in our daily rush to pause and simply be grateful. Religion aside, seeing or holding a newborn baby, seeing a loved one after a time of separation, hearing from clients that they know they are going to be OK—these are the experiences of joy.

Embodiment of Joy

Joy is healing and enlivening and connects us with others, with nature, with life. Because it joins us with our deepest experience—with our own life, our own connectedness with the wider world—it is one of the most precious emotions available to us. In joy, the body is tall yet soft, the eyes are open and moist, the lips are often separated, and the person is generally ready for whatever is about to happen, whether good or bad:

A woman in her 40s told me that her life was increasingly flat and meaningless. I asked her to visit the botanical gardens in Melbourne and to report back on her experience. She returned a week later and told me that the trash bins were overflowing, there were noisy children running unattended, there were weeds in the garden, and the swans and other birds had made messes over paths and seats. I congratulated her on the observations but asked her to return to the gardens, only this time she was to walk a little more briskly, hold her shoulders back a little, and lift her gaze to eye level or a little higher. When she returned the following week, she had a look of amazement on her face and wondered aloud how she had not been able to see previously what she had seen this time. She reported on the beauty of the trees, the height of the gums, the spread of the oaks, the wonderful way the different foliage of the various trees made such a wonderful frame to the sky-line. The lake was expansive, the swans and ducks so active, there was such a variety of ducks and other birds. How had she not seen them before? She hadn't seen them because the way she held her body and the way she walked didn't allow her to see them and to experience them. We speculated about what other aspects of her life she could now enjoy seeing for the first time, and she left excited about exploring the world that had always been there but that she hadn't seen.

EXERCISE 18: FOSTERING
AN ATTITUDE OF JOY

❖ Sit quietly with your hands in an open, receiving position.

❖ Say aloud: "Life may give, life may take, but I am grateful to life, for no good reason, I am grateful to life" (after Julio Olalla).

Pride

We experience pride when our child is successful, when we obtain an academic degree, a new or highly valued car, or computer. As distinct from gratitude and joy, which are emotions related to being given something, pride is related to owning or achieving.

Embodiment of Pride

When we feel pride, we puff out our chest, assume our full height, lift our forehead, and stand solid.

Fun

Fun is an emotion that receives variable appreciation. We experience fun when we are engaged in some activity that has no particular outcome or in which the outcome is not central. Playing golf can be more fun, for example, when we are less concerned with the score and more with the pleasure of being out in the open or sharing the company of a friend. Fun is generally associated with children; many of us

---

EXERCISE 19: GENERATING PRIDE

❖ Stand erect, shoulders back, head up.

❖ Speak aloud or think silently about any number of your achievements or possessions.

❖ Own those achievements or possessions as your legitimately.

❖ Notice how you feel.

learned as part of becoming adult that fun is an emotion to suppress. Look at the faces of commuters on a train on their way home from work and there isn't much fun to observe. Because fun has been associated with children, we can overlook its benefits and associate fun with not being responsible, not being mature. I have noticed recurrently that couples who come to therapy with problems look blank when asked "What do you do for fun?" I have also noticed that one of the most useful interventions for couples is to encourage them to have fun together in whatever form that might take. There is something innately healing about fun, and although it is freely available, there's not a lot of it in obvious use.

Embodiment of Fun

Fun encourages activities that are not directed to some particular outcome, but rather are done for their own sake, "just for fun." That release from the "shoulds," the burdens and pressures of our frantic life these days, can be enlivening, invigorating, and healing.

In such a mood, our body feels lighter and looser, there is a tendency to smile, and all the muscles tend to become more relaxed, more flowing, more supple. It is one of the tragedies of our modern technological life that we have lost contact with this experience; reconnecting with it can make a difference to many of our interactions. Nowhere is this more apparent than in our relationships. Early in an intimate relationship, we have fun, we laugh at nothing and at everything. We go for walks—not to get somewhere, not to lose weight or get fit, but for the pleasure of walking. Later, as routine and burdens set in, walking can itself become a routine and yet another burden, and the fun is lost:

A couple who had been married for 15 years came for separation counseling. They each had their own lawyer and wanted counseling to separate as respectfully and cost-effectively as possible. As we spoke together, I was impressed by the heavy, gloomy mood in the room and asked them if it had always been like this between them. They looked uncertain. I asked them about how they were when they first met, and they looked at each other and smiled with some embarrassment. We discussed what they used to do for fun, how enjoyable that used to be, and how they had somehow got out of the habit of doing those things recently. I suggested that before they went too much further with their divorce, they might want to give the fun one last try.

Even discussing the possibility of fun produced an obvious change in their mood. They became more lively, alert, and attentive to each other. They sat more upright in the chair, their facial expressions softened, and they began to converse about their embarrassment. They were keen to explore this.

The husband phoned to cancel the next appointment, telling me that they preferred instead to go on a cross-country trip, something that they had spoken about years previously but had never gotten around to. I haven't heard from them since, and while it is possible that they didn't make the trip and did get a divorce, I think that it is much more likely that there was a different outcome.

EXERCISE 20: BRINGING FUN BACK INTO YOUR LIFE

❖ Choose an activity that is enjoyable or has been enjoyable in the past.

❖ Create the possibility of enjoyment.

❖ Carry out the activity with no purpose in mind.

❖ Notice your response.

Intimacy

Intimacy is a dilemma for us. It is an emotion in which we risk showing ourselves to another as we are, without pretense or cover. It feels as though we are showing the nakedness of our soul. Intimacy is like air or water; without it, we shrivel and die. At the same time, to be intimate is to open ourselves to the possibility of rejection or damage by the other. It brings the risk of annihilation. So we have this dilemma: without intimacy we might die, but by inviting intimacy we risk death. No wonder it is such a conflicting emotion for us.

To create an experience of intimacy, we simply need to share some personal thought or fear with another. Because this necessitates trust, we need to use caution. How much we are willing to risk ourselves, and so experience intimacy, depends on how trustworthy we assess the other to be. Prudence may be relevant. If there are doubts, perhaps we could begin with some small, relatively safe disclosure, and if that is survived, perhaps we could try something a little more daring. This can help to take care of the worry about jumping into the deep end and risking losing everything.

EXERCISE 21: GENERATING INTIMACY

❖ Choose a partner with whom you feel safe.

❖ Let your body soften, place your hands with palms open and facing upward on your thighs, relax your legs and separate them at the knees, and look your partner in the eyes.

Embodiment of Intimacy

The body is uncertain moving into intimacy, soft and tenta-tive. When the risk is taken, the face softens, the skin glows, the shoulders settle, and there is a gentle smile, perhaps ac-companied by a moistening in the eyes.

Wonderment

What is it to be "moved"? We are moved or touched when we experience being part of something beyond ourselves. When we see a beautiful sunrise or sunset, when we see a new baby, when we actually experience seeing rather than merely recognizing a loved one, when we look at the space between the stars on a clear night we are affected by the experience. Often, our eyes fill up, we feel a sense of be-longing, we can feel a loss of personal boundaries as if we actually begin to blend with the wider experience. Nature provides a permanent source of this emotion, the emotion of spirituality.

We have all experienced at some time the joy of walking in the woods or along the beach on a still or stormy day. It is tempting to overlook the presence of nature and its healing potential because of our preoccupation with activity or the pressure to cope with our increasingly busy lives, yet it can be rewarding to walk in a park or visit some wild place and refresh our soul. Clients complaining of depression or stress or confusion can derive tremendous benefit from opening themselves to some contact with nature, even a small con-tact. When the contact happens, that's when we experience being moved or touched.

Embodiment of Wonderment

In an emotion of wonderment, the body loses its boundaries and disappears as we look outward. The eyes widen, the jaw drops open, the shoulders and torso soften, and we become quietly immobile as we experience being somehow connected with whatever is filling us with wonderment:

At a recent talk on astronomy, the speaker reminded us of the dimensions of the universe—our sun as one of about 100 billion stars in the Milky Way Galaxy, which is one of about 100 billion galaxies. The sheer magnitude was stunning, and the audience was silent and transfixed for a time as the lecture proceeded. The feeling of wonderment is with me as I recall the experience, and I am reminded of it any time I look at the night sky or even think of it.

EXERCISE 22: WONDERMENT

❖ Look at the night sky.

❖ Look at the spaces between the stars.

❖ See that space stretching further than you can imagine.

❖ Feel connected with that space, as if you are part of it, it is part of you.

❖ Notice your experience.

❖ Look at some small stone, leaf, or creature, including a partner, child, or stranger.

❖ Look at the minute details.

❖ Suspend any judgment or assessment.

❖ Feel connected with that object or creature, as if there is no boundary between you and it.

❖ Notice your experience.

Love

So much has been written about love, from classical dramas and sonnets to pop songs. Teenagers swoon over movie idols, people "go crazy" over a new partner as they "fall in love" with each other. But how is this related to love? My favorite definition of love came from Humberto Maturana. He defined love as "the granting of legitimacy to another to live in the world beside us" (1988, p. 246). He distinguishes love from tolerance, in which we accept illegitimate behavior without acting to correct or reform the other.

Granting legitimacy or loving is not to be confused with approval or even liking. We can accept people we love as they are, legitimize them in our experience, and also let them know in the strongest possible terms that their behavior is totally unacceptable. This can help to distinguish the person from his or her actions so that we can love the person and yet despise that person's actions.

I particularly appreciate Maturana's definition because it makes the most precious of our human emotions more accessible, more doable, more attainable. When clients are uncertain about whether they love another, we can ask them if they give the other permission to be who that person is, how that person is, as that person is. If the answer to these questions is yes, we can expect to observe a shift in the emotion of the client in front of our eyes.

Embodiment of Love

In the experience of love, the body softens, the face smoothes out, the breathing slows, the stomach relaxes, and the whole body becomes peacefully disinclined to move—like a body that was hungry for food which has been satiated, or one that was thirsty that has just drank its fill—in the experience of love, the body feels replete and complete, like coming home to itself.

EXERCISE 23: INVITING LOVE

❖ Look at someone or something.

❖ Let your face, eyes, and shoulders soften.

❖ Say silently and sincerely "I give you my permission to be exactly how you are."

❖ Notice how you feel.

Summary

Just as planting a garden with a multitude of plants leaves less room for the weeds, so we can be active gardeners of our own experiences and assist our clients to be more active in nurturing their positive emotions so there is less space for the unwanted varieties. I invite you to reflect on which of these emotions you would like to have more of in your life, recall the body positions and movements accompanying those emotions, place your body in those positions, allow it to move in those ways, and see how that can facilitate the reexperiencing of those emotions. How could you remind yourself to reproduce those emotions that you wanted more of? How could you translate this into your work? When you are working with clients in a counseling conversation, how can you begin to observe their body position and movement, and how might you begin to invite them to shift their position, to move differently so that they are more likely to experience the emotions they want?

CHAPTER FIVE

Strategies in Action

Heinz von Foester, a prominent constructionist, reminds us, "If you desire to see, learn how to act" Paul Watzlawick (1984). I interpret the "act" as having to do with action, not acting lessons. We have all experienced how doing something different changes how we feel about doing it; waiting to become motivated before we begin an activity can take a long time, but motivation frequently arrives as we become involved with that activity. Action, the way we move, can have a profound influence on our experience, and by observing this potential influence and exploring it, we can generate more options for ourselves and for our clients.

When clients come for counseling, they expect a conversation. They expect to tell us some information about the problem—its beginning, its development, what makes it worse, what makes it better—and they expect us to help them look for solutions—understanding, explanation, guidance, ideas—so they can get on with their lives again. There is a strong expectation on both sides of the desk that the process will be verbal and that understanding and insight will be central. This may be usual, but we don't need to limit our approach. There is more than one way to assist clients to get past the roadblock that their problem is causing in their lives.

In previous chapters, we examined the value of asking clients what they like so we can enhance the therapeutic relationship and create rapport and trust. We considered asking about changes that may have begun before clients arrive for their appointments, and that by enhancing these changes, we can move the conversation toward a solution. We saw that when looking for exceptions to the problem situation, by examining times when the problem was not there or not as worrisome, solutions can appear out of the shadows and become visible. We learned the value of the miracle question and how the answer to this question can help the client experience the possibility of life on the other side of the problem. We also saw how crucial it is to identify the degree of engagement clients bring to the counseling session. To help us decide what direction therapy should take we need to determine if clients want to be in counseling; if they recognize that they have a part in finding their solution or if they have been sent to counseling unwillingly; or if they are waiting painfully for a change in weather, government, legal outcome, or personality transplant for their partner to solve the problem.

Because problems are characterized by a paucity of options and solutions are rich in opportunities and choices, we are going to be of most use to our clients if we maintain a collection of methods to help them. If we have only a hammer, we're in trouble if their problem doesn't look much like a nail. If we have a full toolbox, we have a better chance of finding a tool that will satisfy the client and ourselves.

We explored the usefulness of inviting clients to develop a different perspective on their situation, to identify the concern that must always be in the background for a problem to be a problem. We learned that by stating that concern and reframing their problem, we can assist them to change how they view their problem. Now we can investigate ways of altering the *doing* of their problem.

When clients have problems, they are actively doing a series of actions to maintain or even create their problems. These actions are usually so habitual that they are not obvious to the client, although they might be to others. Other family members are predictably aware of the actions of the problem individual even when the individual is blind to it or aggressively denies the existence of such actions.

When we distinguish the specific steps in a problem's sequence, it is usually possible to define a consistent pattern. One of the ways to define a problem is to say that a problem is a problem because of the rigid pattern of actions the client is doing. If we follow this line of thinking, and if we can encourage the client to do different actions, then there will be a different result, and the possibility of a solution can appear. If we assume that a problem is held together tenuously by a delicate network of interconnected actions and that disrupting some or even one of the individual components causes the integrity of the sequence to be lost, the problem can disappear like a burst bubble or can begin to disintegrate like a crumbling building when some critical supporting structure is altered. Asking about the problem in detail can also lead to recognition of exceptions, which can be extended with solution-oriented questioning encouraging the client to continue with and build on what is already working. These interventions can be minor but produce major disruptions.

ALTERING THE *DOING*

If we ask the client in fine detail about the specific steps in the doing of the problem, we can begin to discover *what* happens rather than *why* it happens, and we can begin to generate a map to track the habitual path taken in the problem actions. Once we have a map of the steps taken in the doing of the problem, we can begin to design other ways of doing the actions or create new actions or a new sequence of actions; in other words, we can generate flexibility, variety, and curiosity in the client, which will actively disrupt the problem and allow space for a solution to emerge. These strategic interventions can be designed to alter the sequence of the steps, the rate, the duration, and so on, or alter the background mood. The very act of listening with concern and respect to

---

ALTERING THE *DOING*

Do more of what is working.

Do something different.

Keep a journal.

Break patterns:

❖ Change rate, frequency, timing, duration, location

❖ Add new element

❖ Change sequence

❖ Link complaint to burden

Assign an ambiguous task: "I would like you to find something that symbolizes your problem, carry it around with you for a time, and when you're ready, you'll know what to do with it."

Develop rituals.

---

the problem sequence—the client surviving the telling, the counselor surviving the listening—can be enough to begin to disrupt the habitual mood of self-recrimination in which the client may be trapped.

Do More of What Is Working

Asking about actions that are working for a client can be a simple and elegant way of shifting a client's problem toward a solution. A colleague told me about a client who had been depressed for some time and was not responding to antidepressants. He asked her what she was doing when she was

DO MORE OF WHAT IS WORKING

❖ Ask clients "What are you doing that is helping so far?"

❖ Suggest that they do that as much as convenient.

feeling at her best, and she reported that when she was in the garden she felt fine. He asked her to spend as much time in the garden as possible, and within a short time she reported that she was no longer depressed. She has continued to do more gardening. No one would suggest that gardening is a cure for depression, but in this woman's case, this simple alteration of what she was doing was sufficient. How many others may be able to respond to similar interventions that we haven't explored?

Do Something Different

Couples who are in conflict frequently argue along a well-worn groove of repetition, for example, "If I've told you once, I've told you a thousand times" or "How many more times do I need to tell you that I hate it when you . . ." The sequence is repeated and escalates in the process. I like to ask these couples to do something different in the presence of their partners and, if possible, to keep it a secret. The idea of doing something different can be intriguing to the couple, as they are often bored with the usual routine. Keeping the difference a secret offers an additional benefit: changing the mood from resentment and bitterness to playfulness and mischief. I have seen many times the look of delight on their faces when

---

DO SOMETHING DIFFERENT

❖ Ask clients "What have you been doing that's unhelpful?"

❖ Then ask "What could you do instead of that?"

❖ Offer suggestions for your clients: Could they clean their teeth holding the toothbrush in the opposite hand? Could they drive to work along a different route? Could they park their car in a different place? Could they sit at their meal table in a different chair and perhaps eat something they wouldn't normally eat that would be pleasing?

❖ Ask your clients to notice their experience as they do something different.

---

they contemplate such an opportunity and the relief and gratitude when they return with their relationship renewed and lively:

I asked one couple to save their voices and the furniture by videotaping their next argument. Because all their arguments were simply a variation on the same old theme, future arguments could be circumvented by watching the video together. They didn't get to make the video.

Keep a Journal

We can ask clients to keep a record of their problem before we begin to work on it together; this will give us the data to know how best to proceed. Instruct clients to be certain that they don't make any changes toward solving the problem until we have sufficient information. The injunction to not change anything can release clients from their previous effort to make a change, and the whole process can dissolve. The experience of observing the problem actions can also shift the experience to one that is more objective, more distant. The new observational position can change the observations made and the experiences generated. It is not uncommon for a client to return not with a report, but with a cure:

I asked a shy man in his late 20s to go to as many social events as possible and note how other people coped with their shyness. He was able to report that some were quiet and looked happy with that; others were loud and took center stage and seemed okay about that. I emphasized "seem" and asked him to speculate about what others might have reported if they had been observing him. He wasn't sure, so I asked him to make some more observations. This time he was to observe

---

KEEP A JOURNAL

❖ Ask your clients to make notes about what's happening when the problem is there.

❖ Ask them to make separate notes when the problem isn't there.

❖ Ask them to predict beforehand whether the problem will be there or not, and perhaps the degree of the problem they are anticipating.

❖ Then ask them to compare their predictions and the actual experience and discover something useful.

---

how many people noticed him. He discovered that most people were so involved in their own world that they didn't notice him at all. He was relieved to discover this.

Break Patterns

Once we have a map of the doing of a problem, we can design differences in the rate, frequency, timing, duration, and location of the problem. We can add a new element, change the sequence, or make the problem into an ordeal by linking the unwanted actions to a burden:

A man was complaining that he couldn't control his eating in the evenings even though he was gaining weight. I asked him to eat as much as he wanted, but to keep track of what he ate. He was to set his alarm for 2:30 A.M. and eat a similar amount of food then. From that evening, the thought of eating a similar amount at 2:30 A.M. put him off his appetite.

A young woman had been in therapy for several months to deal with her bulimia. I asked her about the way she stood just before she threw up in the toilet. She looked shocked that I should ask such a personal question. She replied that she just stood. I then asked her how far her face was from the water level in the toilet just before she threw up. She looked even more disgusted with me. She didn't know the distance, so I asked her to feel free to continue her vomiting, but just before the event happened, to estimate the distance between her mouth and the water in the toilet. She reluctantly agreed and on her next visit told me that she knew that I knew that she wouldn't be able to do it. I assured her I had no way of telling the future but was pleased that she had been able to find a way of controlling the habit she had previously been struggling with.

BREAK PATTERNS

❖ Note fine details of the sequence of the problem.

❖ At each step, speculate privately, or with your clients, about what other possible actions *could* follow, and note them down.

❖ Suggest to clients that the next time they begin the problem, they should follow your suggested alternatives, or ask them which they are interested in exploring.

❖ Ask them to notice what is different as they follow the different sequence.

A respectable lawyer was becoming increasingly guilty and confused because, although he wanted to continue his marriage, he was having difficulty ending an affair. I asked him to continue the affair for the time being, and every time he visited his lover, he should leave a $10 bill on the bedside table. He didn't need to do it and ended the affair immediately.

Assign an Ambiguous Task

Some clients remain vague about what would be helpful in solving their dilemma. Therapists may also be uncertain. Instead of insisting on specifics, we can allow for the ambiguity and use it:

A woman in her late 40s was becoming depressed. She had ended a difficult marriage and had completed the divorce but felt that there was something holding her back—something not

---

ASSIGN AN AMBIGUOUS TASK

Ask clients to find something that symbolizes their problem and to carry it around with them for a time. Tell them that when they're ready, they'll know what to do with it.

---

right. I offered her the following: "I would like you to find something that symbolizes your problem, carry it around with you for a time, and when you're ready, you'll know what to do with it." She left in a mood of curiosity and reported two weeks later that when she went home, she noticed the wedding ring she had removed months previously and had placed on her dressing table. This time she really noticed it. She decided to place the ring on the necklace that she always wore. Several days later, she was walking along the beach, not thinking of anything in particular, when she reached up, quickly undid her necklace, removed the ring, and threw it into the sea. She experienced a sense of relief and lightness from that moment.

Develop Rituals

Rituals have been a part of human culture throughout the eons, but with the pace of modern life, they have become less prominent. Yet they still have a place in our experience that can be freeing and healing. Rituals characteristically involve a symbolic object and fire, water, or earth, and are most effective when they provide an opportunity to express through symbolic actions the unwanted or unhelpful emotion that is keeping the problem stuck. If there is resentment, then tearing, burning, or stomping on an object might be helpful. If there is prolonged grief, letting a symbolic object float on a river or out to sea and watching it drift away may give expression to sadness:

A couple came to counseling to repair their marriage. He had had an affair, she found out, and they had a confrontation. Both decided they wanted the marriage to continue, but they questioned how to achieve this genuinely, without regret or ongoing recrimination. I asked them if there was an object that symbolized the affair. The wife's eyes glistened as she said "That tie!!!" The husband was more than a little embarrassed. I asked them what they would like to do with the tie as a symbol of the affair. They spoke together and decided that a ritual burning felt good. They planned to take the tie to a nearby river that night, together pour gas over it, and set it

---

DEVELOP RITUALS

❖ Introduce the idea of a ritual and assess the client's response.

❖ Ask the client what kind of ritual might be useful in the client's particular situation, or suggest some activity involving earth, fire, or water, and ask the client to perform the ritual at a prescribed time and place.

This ritual should give expression to the emotion associated with the problem.

---

alight. After this, they decided to throw the ashes into the river. I invited them to make any sounds or noises they wanted as the tie was burning. They could also say anything to each other as long as the tie was burning. After they had thrown the ashes into the river, they could then feel free of the past and look forward to building the kind of future together that they both wanted.

Conclusion

Altering the doing of a problem can bring strategic interventions to the situation and provide relief when we were previously stuck. The very idea of some of the interventions creates a mood of lightness that helps to shift from the heaviness and resignation often accompanying a problem and can foster solutions in itself. I have heard of concerns for a client's dignity when offered the potential to take some of the seemingly absurd actions we might invent together. This always relates to insufficient attention being given to the therapist-client relationship. It is my consistent experience that clients don't feel manipulated by this seemingly intrusive approach if I respect them. When clients sense that we are concerned about their well-being and helping them to solve their dilemma, that we are attending with care to them as people, it is my experience that clients are relieved to find a way of breaking through the limiting patterns that were causing their suffering, and are delighted to take steps to clear away the obstacles and get on with their life.

Next, we'll focus on some common problems for which clients turn to us for help. By applying what we've learned regarding language, emotions, and the body, we can quickly help clients find solutions to their problems and effect lasting change in their lives.

DEALING WITH STRESS

Stress as a phenomenon has increasingly been claiming our attention. But what is stress? What differentiates stress from tension, depression, feeling stretched, overwhelmed, bored, uncertain, anxious, sad, or experiencing difficulty adapting to change? Can stress be relieved or just managed? Can it be prevented? How can we manage stress in our clients in a clinical setting? How can we learn to manage our own stress? Is it more than eating good food, getting good exercise, and thinking good thoughts? Is it necessary to learn to meditate, or can we design more specific, more easily acceptable, more contemporary measures?

We hear about change everywhere, and of how change is increasing, even accelerating. My father came from Scotland at the age of 14, and only a year later he joined an insurance company. He retired from that same insurance company 50 years later. How many of us will work in the same career for even 20 years? Our children are likely to have many career changes over their working life. We could say we are living in a time of crisis of change.

As a result of this massive change, there is another crisis upon us: a crisis of meaning. This presents tremendous difficulties for us. In *Reality Is Not What It Used to Be* (1990), Walter Truet Anderson, talks of the fragmentation of the past order of things—religion, the family, education, countries—and the pull away from this rapidly approaching chaos and toward fundamentalism. He notes the rise of the fundamentalist Christian churches in Central and South America that had been traditional strongholds of Catholicism, the fundamentalist Islamic movement, and neoconservatism in the United States, Germany, and many other countries around the globe.

Meaning has always been a core concern for us. Viktor Frankl reminds us of its power in *Man's Search for Meaning* (1959). Now there is a deep and wide challenge to meaning, with the postconstructivists challenging the very source of meaning. We could say that one of the crises of the current age is a crisis in meaning itself. It is not surprising, then, that stress appears!

But what is stress? This is a pivotal question to address if we are to provide effective assistance for this ever increasing problem.

Everyone's Stress Is Different

I have found it helpful to put aside my understanding of stress and instead ask clients for details of their own personal experience. When I ask such questions, clients answer with comments such as "I feel overwhelmed, confused, sad; I am uncertain about coping with change; I don't know how to manage; I don't know what to do about my teenage child's behavior." These comments tend to have a more everyday mood about them. Frequently, just voicing this description of stress, which is the client's and not mine, can itself lessen the intensity of the client's experience of the stress and make it more manageable.

The label "stress" is amorphous. When it is exchanged for "sad," "not coping," "overwhelmed," and so forth, the situation becomes less scary because these are experiences we have all had and dealt with in varying degrees. When stress translates into sadness, we can explore the sadness: Is it healthy and understandable after the loss of a loved one, for example? Sometimes this exploration is sufficient to deal with the stress; the client can recognize it and say with relief "So, it's all right for me to feel sad, isn't it?" Clients complaining of feeling stressed from not coping are often

---

QUESTIONS TO DEFINE THE CLIENT'S
EXPERIENCE OF STRESS

❖ What is stress to you?

❖ If you were to use another word to describe your situation, what would that be?

❖ Stress is a word, and like any word has different meaning for different people. What does it mean to you?

❖ How does your experience of stress interfere with your life? How does it limit you?

---

relieved to discover that what they are trying to cope with is not unique—many others may also be coping with similar problems—or that their reaction may be a normal reaction to an abnormal situation: Who wouldn't be upset if your loved one died, if you lost your job, or if your teenager ran away? Just realizing this can reduce the intensity of the unwanted experience:

A woman was referred to me for stress management. She had facial pain following dental work six months previously and was increasingly tearful and unable to cope with her children, her husband, her work, and life generally. She was diagnosed with psychosomatic pain due to her stress.

After a second opinion from another dentist, she discovered that her pain was a result of a root abscess, and after adequate dental treatment, the pain subsided. She said she was still stressed. When I asked her what the word stress meant to her, she pondered and then replied that she had lost faith in her family because they doubted her pain, and the health professionals who had labeled her neurotic.

Her stress was an issue of damaged trust. I assured her that her reaction was absolutely understandable given the situation she was in, that she had experienced a normal reaction to abnormal circumstances. She was relieved to hear that and visibly relaxed.

We then spoke about trust: how she made the judgment about trusting someone; how she had previously dealt with disappointment when someone had broken her trust; how her gut feelings about the original dentist had her doubt his ability and how she could pay more attention to her intuition in the future and give her own judgment more trust; how important it was to not trust blindly, to not be naïve; how to rebuild trust or end a relationship when trust is too severely damaged. This was a useful learning experience for her, and she stated that she now felt able to deal with trust issues with more confidence and less fear.

Her stress was resolved by first identifying what stress meant to her and then dealing more directly with her experience while avoiding the disconnecting problem of being labeled. She was able to draw on her previous experiences and deal with her present stress and also readied herself for handling future stresses.

When clients suffering from stress state that they are feeling overwhelmed, first suggest ways to alleviate the symptoms: by finding support, offloading some duties, learning to not take on new pressures. Also, by asking for the

ALTERNATIVE DESCRIPTIONS OF STRESS		
Overwhelmed	Sad	Tense
Trying to cope with change	Too busy	Bored
Depressed	Not challenged	Confused
Feeling lost	Frustrated	Hopeless
Directionless	Panicky	Insecure
Anxious	Lonely	Trapped
Guilty	Ashamed	Burdened
Disorganized	Overtired	

client's definition of stress, the counseling process can be tailored to fit the individual and so be more effective.

Normalizing Stress

Aldous Huxley said that experience isn't what happens to us, but what we do to what happens to us. When we are experiencing a situation that might be called stressful, there is a conversation running in the background that this should not be happening, that we are unique and probably abnormal. Genuinely validating the legitimacy of the client's experience can make a difference. A comment such as "It seems to me that you are having a perfectly normal reaction to an abnormal situation" can be very reassuring to a client. If it is appropriate, it can also be helpful to say "I had a similar experience myself and I'm not sure I did as well as you are doing" or "Given the circumstances, I think you should be congratulated for doing as well as you are."

NORMALIZING STRESS

❖ It seems to me that you are having a perfectly normal reaction to an abnormal situation.

❖ I had (or I have known others who have had) a similar experience and I'm not sure I (or they) did as well as you are doing.

❖ Given the circumstances, I think you should be congratulated for doing as well as you are.

What's behind the Stress?

The background concern that is generating clients' stress is usually easily related to their individual definitions of stress. For example, if the definition is "feeling overwhelmed," the concern is likely to be about needing to have more time for the self, fewer obligations at work or home—in other words, "underwhelmed." If it is "tense," the concern might be for greater relaxation. If it is "too busy," the concern might be to have more "down" time.

Asking the question "What is the concern?" instead of "What's wrong that needs to be fixed?" takes the conversation directly toward resolving the dilemma and frequently leads toward a solution, adding to the effectiveness of the conversation as well as saving much time. Simply stating the concern is validating for the client and often deeply consoling. If a client says she is stressed about her new job, and we ask what that means to her, she may respond by saying that there are a lot of new activities to learn. The counselor can then normalize the source of stress and help the client

New Definition of Stress	What's the Concern?
Overwhelmed	More time, more support, less work
Tense	Relaxation
Too busy	Time to do nothing
Confused	Direction, clarity
Panicky	Peace
Overtired	Rest
Fearful	Security
Trying to cope with change	Learning to cope with change
Lonely	Company
Depressed	Feeling more cheerful
Bored	Interests
Not challenged enough	Challenge
Worried	Trust in the future
Guilty	Self-forgiveness
Ashamed	Acceptance
Resentful	Forgiveness of another
Resigned	Generating future possibilities
Procrastination	Taking action
Helpless	Self-help
Hopeless	Hope
Out of control	Sense of control

recognize that a new job brings with it new activities and so it's not surprising that she hasn't settled in fully yet. This reassurance can be furthered by asking more about the client's concern. For example, the client might recognize that doing her job well is a concern. The counselor can offer reassurance by saying, "You must be a conscientious worker because only people who are concerned about the quality of their work would have this concern." This simple, undeniable statement not only affirms the legitimacy of the client's problem but can dissolve the problem at the same time. The ground shifts from "I'm defective because I have this problem" to "I'm a conscientious person," and it would be difficult for the client to have a problem with that!

EXERCISES TO RELIEVE STRESS

❖ Ask "What is *stress* to you?"

❖ Define the concern generating the stress.

❖ Validate the legitimacy of the concern (normalize and reframe).

❖ What emotion is fueling the stress?

❖ What emotion would you prefer?

❖ How could you have more of that emotion? Ask the client to notice when he or she is already feeling the emotion.

❖ What is your body doing when you are experiencing stress?

❖ What would you prefer your body to do?

❖ How could you promote that?

Conclusion

Asking each client how stress affects him or her personally and then looking for the concern behind the problem provide the opportunity to more rapidly and effectively address the problem. The use of these questions can add solidity to the client's capacity to deal with stress. By affirming clients' strengths by discovering their background concern, clients are validated and enabled to cope with future stresses.

TREATING DEPRESSION WITHOUT GETTING DEPRESSED

Recent epidemiological studies confirm what most mental health professionals already suspect: the rate of depression is rising. Depression as a phenomenon is increasingly getting our attention. But what is depression?

We saw in the previous section that different people experience stress differently. The same is true for depression, and reminding ourselves of this keeps us focused on the individual and prevents us from getting lost in the theoretical texts about conditions and syndromes. I find it useful to remind myself that I am never dealing with stress, depression, or any "condition," but always with a person. The brochure for the First International Congress on Ericksonian Approaches to Hypnosis and Psychotherapy in 1980 included this observation from Milton Erickson: "Each person is an individual. Hence, psychotherapy should be formulated to meet the uniqueness of the individual's needs, rather than tailoring the person to fit the Procrustean bed of a hypothetical theory of human behaviour."

Everywhere we hear about the shortage of time. Counselors, along with many small businesses, are finding they need to work longer hours with less support for a lower income and with no relief in sight. Signs point to a continuation of this trend. Parents find themselves overloaded with responsibilities—earning income, paying the mortgage, driving children here and there—and there is an increasing shortage of time for the marriage and family relationships.

Paralleling this time scarcity is a growing feeling of disconnectedness. With the increasing pace of change and life in general, and the resulting pressures, it is easy to put importance on achievement, acquiring material possessions, results—getting to where we are going—at the expense of our experience of the journey, the people in our lives, our neighbors, our community, the world around us. We all know we should "stop and smell the roses," but do we have the time?

It's not surprising, then, that there is a mood of resignation in the air, a mood of acceptance that this is how things are, and although we don't like it, we feel powerless to influence things, and in any case things aren't going to change! This mood of resignation and sense of helplessness over events, the disconnectedness in our social environment, the scarcity of time—these are the ingredients for the spreading phenomenon that has been labeled *depression.*

How can we manage depression in our clients in a clinical setting? How can we learn to manage our own depression? Is it more than finding the right antidepressant, eating right, getting good exercise, and thinking good thoughts?

Although it is important to remember that each individual's experience of depression is unique, we can make some general observations about clients who are depressed. Clients suffering from depression often exhibit predictable fixation and frequent ruminations on past events; if clients are able to foresee any future for themselves at all, it is viewed as an extension of the hopeless past in which they felt helpless to change things for the better. It is relevant here to look for ways of orienting the client to the future, and rather than ruminating on past causes, to initiate some actions for change.

The newer, so-called clean antidepressants are becoming more popular, but some question whether they are sufficient to deal with this problem. But what is the problem, exactly? There is a tremendous lack of consistency in theories about the nature and causes of depression. Some insist on a biological explanation, others sociological, others intrapsychic. With so many disparate explanations and theories, how do we begin to treat depression? There is also increasing dissatisfaction with pushing pills as a panacea. No one who has seen the dramatic mood shift from overwhelming helplessness to hope and possibility can doubt their effectiveness, but are they sufficient? Cloe Madanes wrote in her characteristically incisive way, "Satisfying human relationships can be the most healing 'medications' of all. No amount of exercise, meditation, massage, stress reduction or broccoli is an adequate substitute for love and affection for promoting health" (1999, p. 44).

Whether or not antidepressants are prescribed, there are ways we can usefully interact with our clients to restore their sense of adequacy as humans and to help them generate a more optimistic future. Erickson stated in the foreword to "Change" (1974) that in his experience, people sought help for their problems not because of the unchangeable past, but because of discontent with the present and a desire for a better future. Nowhere is this more applicable than to the dilemma of treating depression. We can design conversations so the better future our depressed clients desire is made more attainable, more accessible, and more available to them. These conversations follow the general principles outlined earlier in this book and emphasize the generative nature of language and conversations. Because some conversations can be harmful and others can be healing, it is important that we do what we can to foster healing conversations.

One of life's ongoing lessons is its unpredictability. The vast majority of depression problems resolve themselves or are attended to by family or friends. The other end of the dilemma is that whatever our level of skill and goodheartedness, there will always be those we are unable to help. Recognizing this can help mental health professionals from becoming depressed ourselves. We can only do what we can, and that can be enhanced by attending to some general principles.

Depression Is Different for Different People

As counselors, we must include in our general understanding of depression the clients' details of their own personal experience with depression.

Depression can be similar to stress. When I ask clients to describe their depression, they answer with comments such as "I feel overwhelmed, confused, sad; I am uncertain about coping with change; I don't know how to manage; I don't know what to do about my teenage child's behavior." Just as in dealing with clients coping with stress, we try to normalize the feelings of depression. Showing clients that their

---

QUESTIONS TO DEFINE THE CLIENT'S EXPERIENCE OF DEPRESSION

❖ What is depression to you?

❖ If you were to use another word to describe your situation, what would that be?

❖ Depression is a word, and like any word has different meaning for different people. What does it mean to you?

❖ How does your experience of depression interfere with your life? How does it limit you?

comments are not so different from what other people experience can lessen the intensity of the experience and make it more manageable. As when helping clients deal with stress, it is important that the definition of depression be the client's and not the clinician's.

When depression translates into being overwhelmed, we can explore the overwhelming feeling: Is it perhaps healthy and understandable, given the client's life situation? Sometimes this exploration is in itself sufficient to deal with the depression and the client can recognize and say with relief "So, it's all right for me to feel overwhelmed, isn't it?" To invite a client to consider that any normal person would feel overwhelmed in such a situation can be healing. Normalizing the situation, if it can be sincerely and coherently normalized, can lead to the dissolution of the problem.

When clients suffering from depression state that they feel hopeless, we can help them find ways out of their dilemma,

---

ALTERNATIVE DESCRIPTIONS OF DEPRESSION

Overwhelmed	Hopeless	Sad
Tense	Helpless	Stressed
Trying to cope with change	No time	Inadequate
Bored	Not challenged	Confused
Feeling lost	Frustrated	Hopeless
Directionless	Panicky	Insecure
Anxious	Lonely	Trapped
Guilty	Ashamed	Burdened
Disorganized	Overtired	Resigned

ask how they have found hope in previous "hopeless" situations, and identify who could assist them. By asking for the client's individual definition of depression at the point of treatment, the counseling process can be tailored to fit the individual so that it is more effective.

Normalizing Depression

When clients experience depression, they can do without the added burden of a crippling label or a daily reminder of their "condition." Anything we can do to relate their experience to everyday life experiences will help them to reconnect with their resources—those they aren't using that could help neutralize the problem.

Finding What's Missing

In the section on stress, we explored the value of asking the client "What's missing for you that, if it were present, would make the problem go away?" It can be helpful to ask the

---

NORMALIZING DEPRESSION

❖ I'm not sure if you're depressed or having a healthy response to an unhealthy occurrence.

❖ If any other normal person had experienced what you have experienced, I would expect that they might have a similar response to yours.

❖ Given the situation you've been in, some people might say that you are coping surprisingly well.

same question to clients experiencing depression. The answer is usually related to the new direction and actions needed to relieve the depression. For example, if the definition of depression is "There are no possibilities for me," what's missing is likely to be about possibilities. If it is "I feel guilty," what's missing is self-forgiveness. If it is "I feel inadequate," what's missing might be feelings of personal adequacy or self-acceptance.

As noted earlier, asking the question "What's missing?" instead of "What's wrong that needs to be fixed?" takes the conversation directly toward exploring some action to be taken and frequently leads toward a solution, adding to the effectiveness of the conversation as well as saving much time. Recognizing and accepting that something is missing is validating for the client and often deeply consoling. If a client states he is depressed about a relationship ending, and we ask what's missing for the client, he may respond that he needs to accept the reality. By normalizing the experience, we can then help to focus the client's attention on what is a useful direction to follow. The experience shifts from I'm defective, and should be coping better, to I'm having a normal reaction, and I can begin to do what is helpful to me for my future. A client can be expected to appreciate this new and useful direction, which comes from them, in the conversation that we foster. Refer also to "New Definition of Stress" p. 135.

NEW DEFINITION OF DEPRESSION	WHAT'S MISSING?
Hopeless	The possibility of a better future.
Helpless	What action to begin to take.

Conversations to Help Healing

Earlier in the book, we learned the value of asking clients for information about times when they weren't experiencing the problem. As humans, we are naturally limited by our biology, which is very accomplished at accommodating experiences. We can smell a rose, hear a sound, feel a sensation for only a limited time before our nervous system becomes desensitized and the smell, sound, or sensation blends with the background and becomes unnoticeable. Asking clients to become aware of these previously unnoticed experiences can facilitate their search for a satisfactory solution.

This process is further enhanced if we ask clients about their experience in less technical and more everyday terms. Clients are more likely to be able to recall, or notice in the future, a time when they were feeling less *sad,* less *overwhelmed,* or less *troubled* than times when they were less *depressed.* By changing the label from depression to sadness or a feeling of being overwhelmed, we lessen the drama, bring the experience to ground, and invite a more everyday kind of connection, and so make the solution more available.

We can ask clients the miracle question—What would happen if the depression were to suddenly lift?—and then look with them for any early hints of this happening so we can enhance these glimpses in our conversations together. Again, this is likely to be more useful and translate more readily into the client's life if we can bring terms more common than "depression" to the conversation.

Between sessions, we can ask clients to be more vigilant about noticing specific times when they feel less sad, less overwhelmed, or less troubled. When they return for their next visit, we will have some relevant questions to ask to bring these more desirable experiences into the foreground and work them into our clients' experience so they have relevance and meaning to them. I have noticed that this process helps the solution stick and facilitates future crisis resolution and even prevention.

The Embodiment of Depression

Depressed clients are characteristically inactive and experience low energy levels. Their shoulders may be slumped forward, their gaze downcast, their expressions flat. Talking about their past, their problems, their feelings will predictably accentuate all these bodily responses and so is best avoided.

To combat these symptoms, we can encourage physical activity, perhaps accompanying the client on a walk along the street or, even better, through a nearby park. Encourage them to look ahead, even upward, asking them to notice the sky, the kinds of clouds, details about a bird or tree, whatever requires that they lift their head and direction of vision.

Conclusion

Asking clients how depression affects them personally and then looking for what's missing to solve the problem offers the opportunity to more rapidly and effectively address their problem. The use of these questions can add a solidness to the experience of being more capable of dealing with the depression. When we affirm their strengths, our clients are validated and enabled to cope with future depression.

FOSTERING HEALTHY RELATIONSHIPS

We Are Relating Beings

We are in a multitude of relationships: with parents, life and business partners, family members, staff, clients, neighbors, other road users, nature—even with ourselves. Wherever we look, we can see relationships.

When our relationships are going well, we are going well; when any of our relationships are not going well, the dilemma can percolate into all areas of our life. We can wake up on top of the world one fine spring morning, but then our first client says something unpleasant, complains about the receptionist, our treatment, or the client's worsening problem, and suddenly winter arrives: the sun goes behind clouds, the cold front appears, rain and sleet are everywhere. The mood we had on waking has dispersed and we know we were mistaken; the world isn't a lovely place at all, and the main problem with the world is the people in it. Later in the morning, a client makes a favorable comment, is doing surprisingly well, is appreciative, and again the weather changes: the sun is out again and the world glows. All these changes are changes in our experience, in our mood, in our life. All are profoundly influenced by the shift in our relationships—a shift in our relating.

We see in some of our clients, and if we dared to look we might see in some of our own experiences, that we can even be influenced by relationships with those who died years ago, or those on the other side of the planet, or even with those who don't exist! We are capable of having a miserable life waiting for Ms. or Mr. Right or waiting for the metamorphosis of our spouse into the right spouse. How many more times do we need to instruct them about how they should be? Don't they know that if they made the changes they would also benefit? Why can't they see that we are asking for their own good? No wonder divorce and family breakups, with all the associated suffering and anguish, are rampant.

We can resent how our parents related to us or how they didn't relate to us decades previously. Even though there is nothing we can do to correct this, we see clients, and perhaps ourselves, who wither and die emotionally while clinging to resentment. Physically, resentment ravages our stomach as ulcerations, our circulatory system as coronary arterial disease, our immune system in a variety of illnesses, our lungs as asthma. We find ourselves living increasingly disconnected lives in an increasingly disconnected society where drugs and addictions of all kinds abound.

Relationships Are in Crisis

Everywhere we look, we see the ravages of failed or unsatisfying relationships: in our clients, our own families, our environment, even among nations. Counseling itself is under stress because of unsatisfactory relationships with our clients, our peers, and government regulatory bodies.

Even though we are relating beings, even though we want to get on well with our family, our staff, our clients, our community, our environment, other countries, we humans do not have a good history of relating. Personal bickering, professional infighting, environmental abuse, and international conflict seem to be constants in our history on this planet. A variety of solutions is offered to us: traditional religious approaches; personal growth workshops; and counseling that recommends acceptance, tolerance, defending personal rights, and so forth. Although each of these can be helpful and relevant at times, we can hardly expect that any single approach will adequately deal with all problems of relating.

We can begin to deal with this central problem by daring to genuinely recognize that we actually don't know what to do. When we have a hammer, a lot of nails suddenly appear; in the same way, fundamentalism is seductive in times of rapid change such as our present era. Instead, we need to diversify the number of tools available to us and refrain from forcing problems to "fit" our existing modes of treatment:

A couple asked for counseling because of problems in their marriage of 17 years. She wanted a divorce because she was tired of waiting for him to change, and he wanted the marriage to continue because he had hope that she would eventually grow to accept him. They each had made an appointment with their own lawyer and they brought an atmosphere of tension into the room with them. She proceeded to list his defects while he expressed hurt and disappointment about her failure to recognize that he was at least trying. They were resentful and resigned about their situation. Divorce seemed imminent.

I asked them to look silently at each other for a time and begin to wonder who the person was they were looking at. They certainly were not seeing who was there; they were too busy looking for who was not there, who should be there, who could be there. I asked them to ponder silently about who this person was they were looking at. They were surprised, then shocked and embarrassed as they recognized that they had ceased seeing their spouse years previously and were totally unaware of whom they were with.

I asked them to spend some time together discovering from whom they were going to get divorced, because it was obvious to me, and it was becoming increasingly obvious to them, that they did not know! I received a phone call a week later informing me that they intended to be solidly married, perhaps for the first time.

Reconnecting from Disconnection

In our busy lives, with increasing pressures from all directions, it is easy, perhaps even necessary, to disconnect from others simply to get through the day. We have clients to see, reports to write, practice management issues to deal with, and then there are the journal articles, the world news, the home accounts. How can we see the devastation of war and stay connected to the experience? To do so would demand that we put aside the relative pettiness of our personal concerns and actually do something about the situation. By staying disconnected, we can maintain our stability and see the suffering as if it is happening to "them," not "us." Our clients suffer from similar pressures and these same feelings of disconnectedness. Before long, some busy couples might make an appointment to see us because that will be the only occasion they can schedule in their frantic lives to even have an argument.

We can recognize the disconnection, but what can we do to reconnect? What follows are two exercises I have found to be helpful with couples who want to repair or enhance their relationships. Both are silent exercises, which can be a relief when couples get into an argument trying to "talk about their problem." You may wish to try either or both of these exercises the next time you find yourself working with a couple or with your own life partner.

EXERCISE: GETTING IN SYNC

❖ Arrange the seating so the couple are facing each other squarely.

❖ Ask the husband to attend to the blinking of his wife's eyes and match his own eye blinks to his wife's blinking rate.

❖ At the same time, ask the wife to attend to the breathing of her husband and match her own breathing to her husband's breathing rate.

❖ This should be done in silence perhaps for as long as two or three minutes before the roles are reversed—the wife matches the husband's blinking while the husband matches the wife's breathing— again for several silent minutes.

After the initial embarrassment, there is often a mood of lightness and even hilarity as the previously arguing individuals share the experience of being with the other genuinely, connectedly, and relating.

Again, there is frequently a delight in the freshness and genuineness of the interaction, uncontaminated by words and expectations. Often, a mood of appreciation, lightness, and even joy can be generated, providing relief from previous tension that can become infectious.

Find Out What's Already Working Some of the Time

If we ask about the times when things are going at their best, or when they are at least not so bad, we can frequently assist the couple to clarify for themselves what does work for

---

EXERCISE: DANCING WITH THE HANDS

❖ Ask the couple to stand silently facing each other, looking into each other's eyes, and to lift their hands so their fingertips are lightly touching the fingertips of their partner.

❖ Ask each to begin to move their left hand in a gentle and random manner so their right hand is led by their partner.

❖ Ask them to play with the movements, to see what are the limits in various directions, all performed in silence to enhance the ability to connect with the other directly, not only through words.

❖ If they are interested, they can let other parts of their body join in, perhaps their hips, their feet, and even their whole body. Some music can help here.

them so they can do more of that and as a result have fewer problem times.

Preappointment Changes

When a couple arrive with a genuine desire to work on their problem, start by asking them about changes that have already happened since they made the appointment. It is not uncommon to hear the couple speak about some useful changes; perhaps they began to talk about why the appointment was made or what they wanted to have happen in the appointment, perhaps just sitting down together and discussing something—in this case, the problem. Often, the couple are surprised to recognize that things have begun to change. Pointing this out can be a stepping stone to inquiring about how they might do more of this in the future.

Ask about Likes

Next, ask what the couple like to do together for fun. If they have no time together, ask if there were any fun times in the past. If so, ask how they could start up those activities they had gotten out of the habit of doing together. It may be something as simple as walking around the block together on a Sunday morning, reading the paper together, or sitting down together for a cup of tea. If the couple cannot remember any fun times in the past, ask what they might begin to do together that could be enjoyable and fun for both rather than a chore.

The Miracle Question

If we find ourselves confronted with the couple who can't move forward in therapy, we can pop the miracle question: If, when you were both asleep tonight, the problem just vanished (yet because you were asleep, you wouldn't know just how it happened), and when you woke up in the morning

---

QUESTIONS FOR COUPLES

❖ What did you do together when you first met that was fun for you both?

❖ What did you do for fun before this problem came into your life?

❖ What do your friends do for fun?

❖ What will be the first thing you could enjoy together when this problem begins to get sorted out?

❖ Which of your friends/family will be the first to notice that you are enjoying things together again?

❖ Do something special for your partner, but try to keep it a secret.

❖ See if you can guess or anticipate the fun activity your partner will try to keep secret from you.

---

things were more or less as you would hope for in your relationship, what would be different? How would you know things were different? Who would be the first to notice, you or your partner? These kinds of questions can help to focus the direction of the counseling process and at the same time keep it realistic and achievable.

Whatever ideas the couple come up with in response to this question, the counselor can extend the experience by asking if there are any hints of those changes already present, although perhaps not noticed until now. The inquiry itself helps to shift the direction from criticism and resentment to a joint curiosity and alignment of purpose.

Between-Session Homework

However the session progresses, we can ask the couple to notice certain things between now and the next appointment. If they have identified some activities they want to do more of, we can ask them to do more of those things and notice the result. If they can't come up with any ideas, we can ask them to notice anyway, just in case something good happens, as it would be a shame to let it pass unnoticed. It can also be valuable to give each member of the couple the task of noticing what aspects of their partner they *don't* want to change, what about their partner they already appreciate very much.

What If the Couple Aren't Willing?

Sometimes, one partner (the complainant) brings the other, complaining that he or she is the problem, while the brought partner doesn't want to be in counseling at all (in other words, is a visitor). It is essential in this situation to first notice that the couple are not actively and usefully engaged in the conversation and then invite them into a different kind of interchange, one that has at least a chance of leading to a solution. To acknowledge the complainant's complaint as legitimate and difficult to deal with can draw that person into the conversation instead of existing around the edge of it, and legitimizing the brought partner's reluctance to be present can also make a difference. We then have the possibility of working with a minimally interested couple to discover what small changes they are willing to make, what small compromises they are willing to declare, or what attribute of the other they are willing to admit. This can provide a subtle and sometimes dramatic change in the mood and direction of the counseling session.

Exercises to Regenerate Relationships

Questions

When did you first fall in love?

What was it about your partner that let you know he or she was the one for you?

What have you discovered in your relationship so far that you would share with your children to help with their relationships?

What are the three or four most important contributions your partner has made to you?

Which shared experiences will be most memorable in your old age?

Which of your faults has your partner shown the most tolerance of?

How do you explain your partner's ability in this area?

Emotions

How would you recognize a feeling of love for your partner?

How would you recognize a feeling of love from your partner?

How have you managed to dare to let your partner see who you really are?

The Body

How can you sit/stand/be with your partner so that he or she can best recognize his or her true feelings of appreciation of you?

What can you enjoy doing together?

When was the last time you danced/walked holding hands/sang a song together?

Relationships: The Human Mystery

We can offer much to our clients to assist them in learning how to have relationships that are more mutually satisfying, nurturing, and lively. Yet within the enormous complexity of the human condition, the most we can offer is assistance. No one has or ever will have a simple answer to this most complex of human circumstances, but by respecting the individual's uniqueness, working with each individual couple to help them find their own solutions, encouraging them to do less of what doesn't work and more of what does work, we can foster an appreciation of the profound mystery of human relationships.

GETTING TO SLEEP WHEN YOU CAN'T

"I Can't Relax"

A woman in her early 20s had trouble going to sleep because of worrying thoughts about her new job. Would she be up to it? Would the boss like her? Would she get on with her new workmates? These thoughts went round and round and she had difficulty "turning off" at night.

Turning off, winding down, slowing down are increasing problems in our accelerating world. There is increasing pace and pressure wherever we look. Even elementary school children are suffering from difficulties going to sleep because of tests or an approaching school camp. We need to find a way to break the cycle of worrying, leading to staying awake, leading to worrying about staying awake. For small children, we sing them a song or tell them a story, and this does the trick. For older children or adults, some variations on this theme are just as helpful.

When my teenage children complain that they can't sleep, I've frequently suggested that instead of trying to go to sleep, they close their eyes and try to stay awake. Mostly they can't. Other children and young adults have reported similar benefits. Reversing the problem paradox from "The harder I try to sleep, the wider awake I become" to a therapeutic paradox, "The harder I try to stay awake, the sleepier I become," is likely to help because the client is already thinking this way and the intervention merely reverses the process.

In our instant fix society, there is a seductive pull toward a magic pill that will dissolve all our cares, relax our troubled brow, and put us to sleep. But when we give the experience over to an external agent, we deprive ourselves of the opportunity to learn something for ourselves. A further concern is that medication can lead to dependency and inadvertently make the situation worse, requiring escalating doses with diminishing results.

When we are tense, it is more difficult to fall asleep than when we are relaxed. There are exercises to help clients achieve a more relaxed state so that they are more able to fall asleep naturally. We can ask clients to sit back in their chair, gently allow their eyes to close, and begin to focus on their feet. We can suggest that they let their feet relax comfortably, naturally, taking their own time. We can then suggest that the feeling of relaxation (or is it comfort, or security, or ease?) begin to spread throughout their physical experience. It may spread slowly or rapidly, in a linear or random fashion. We can suggest that they enjoy the experience, learn how it is for themselves, so they can recall the experience at some future time when it will be useful—perhaps at some time of stress, perhaps as they are going to sleep tonight, perhaps at some other time.

We can assist clients to learn how to have an imagined relaxing experience by suggesting that they sit in the chair in our office, close their eyes, and go to some pleasing, relaxing place—perhaps the beach, perhaps the woods, perhaps some other place they choose. It is better to let the client choose the place so that the counselor doesn't inadvertently choose one with unpleasant associations. For example, asking someone to relax near the beach might bring back a memory of when that person or someone else nearly drowned. Asking the client to go for a pleasant walk in a field of wheat might precipitate an acute asthma attack if the client is allergic to wheat.

Give the client open-ended suggestions, such as *I'd like you to get comfortable, let your eyes close when you're ready, and let your mind drift to a place where you can relax and feel safe. I don't need to know where that place is, but you can find it easily and pleasantly. When you find that place, I'd like you to settle into the experience of being there and begin to look around and see all there is to see. Perhaps you notice something about the air that is relaxing. Is it the freshness, the clarity? Is there a perfume on the air, perhaps the smell of the sea, perhaps the smell of pine, perhaps something else? What sounds can you begin to notice? How does it feel in your body to be here in this wonderful place, where you can relax, free from all the worries and cares of the world?*

It is usual for clients to be observably relaxed at this stage, their facial muscles looser, their breathing slower and deeper, a relative stillness apparent in their body. It can be helpful to ratify these changes by commenting on them to make them more noticeable to the client: *As I've been talking to you, your muscles have relaxed, the circulation in the skin of your face has changed, your breathing has changed to be slower and deeper, and your body is demonstrating the stillness of someone who is learning to relax.*

Physical relaxation produced by progressively or randomly suggesting that clients relax the muscles of their body can also be beneficial: *I don't know if it will be your feet that will relax more easily than your hands, whether your face will become more comfortable than your breathing, whether your stomach will feel as if it is softening in a reassuring, comforting way, or whether you will feel more as you would like to feel as you gently and naturally drift into a soothing and restful sleep.*

We can then ask clients to take note of their experience and learn it: *When you are ready to go to sleep tonight, you can close your eyes, recall this pleasant place, which is your place, and notice all that you can notice as you drift off into a natural, refreshing sleep.* This simple experience, which may take as long as 10 minutes, can break the worry cycle and allow clients to return to their normal sleeping pattern. Helping clients to relax is a productive way to handle the vast majority of sleeping problems, particularly if they are introduced early in a client's sleeplessness, before a habit of expecting sleeplessness settles in with all the possible sequelae, such as depression, anxiety, and so on.

"Relaxing Doesn't Help"

A woman in her mid-50s had been recently widowed, and although she had accepted her husband's death with relief after his long illness from colon cancer, her life seemed empty, and she was wondering what she was going to do with the rest of her life. She had tried relaxation exercises and discovered that "the more relaxed I become, the more wide awake I am!"

Her problem was worrying too much. Relaxing her muscles, thinking of something pleasant was not relevant here. She had tried it and it didn't help. Following the maxim "If it works, do it; if it doesn't work, do something different," I reframed her problem by offering the idea that her worrying could serve a useful purpose. She clearly had to find a different way of living now that she was alone. I suggested that she really did need to do some serious thinking. We negotiated a "thinking period" of 30 minutes each night; I asked her to actively worry with her eyes closed for 30 minutes when she first went to bed, and if she was still awake then, perhaps she could get out of bed and write her worries down.

When she realized that the worrying had a function, she was able to stop worrying about the worrying. Usually, she didn't last the 30 minutes of prescribed worrying but just went to sleep. If she needed to get up and write, she saw this as useful and again didn't have conflict about it. Within several weeks the whole problem wound down, and she was back to a normal sleeping pattern, but with some useful working out done about her new future.

Milton Erickson pioneered the use of ordeals to help clients overcome their difficulties. He devised activities associated with problems so that clients found themselves preferring to not do the problem to avoid the ordeal. For example, in the wonderful video, *The Artistry of Milton H. Erickson, M.D.* (1975), a widower had been sleeping only two hours a night for years. He lived with his son and they shared the housework. It was his job to polish the floor—a job he loathed. Erickson told him he could cure his insomnia if he would be willing to sacrifice eight hours of sleep. The man was glad to forsake this. He was instructed to get out the floor wax at his normal time for going to bed, and instead of trying to sleep he was to polish the floor until it was time to get up. He could then dress and go to work. He would have lost only two hours of sleep. On the third night, he told his son he was going to lie down to rest his eyes for a moment. He woke up eight hours later. Erickson told him to keep that floor wax by his bed, and any time he had difficulty going to sleep, he was to polish the floor all night long. Erickson reported that he hadn't missed a night's sleep since.

Such an "ordeal" must be beneficial to the client, never punitive or cruel. (The floor did need polishing at some time.) Following Erikson's example, when a client asks me for help with sleeping and if the client has tried relaxation without benefit, I like to ask "What do you hate doing most around the house?" I listen for an activity that is quiet and unlikely to disturb others. Asking someone to vacuum the house at 2 A.M. is not acceptable if there are other people living there. This hated activity can then be linked with not sleeping by suggesting the client perform the ordeal if he or she is not asleep in 30 minutes, 5 minutes, an hour, or whatever the client says is a reasonable time. This will vary considerably from client to client.

"I Just Can't Get to Sleep, No Matter What I Try"

A man in his late 30s consulted me because when he went to bed, instead of going to sleep he would toss and turn for a while, then in desperation, he'd get up, go to the kitchen, make a cup of coffee, read a book for half an hour or so, and then go back to bed. Usually, he would be able to sleep then.

When I asked him what he hated most, he reported that he was studying French and although he loved the study, there were some irregular verbs that were difficult and boring to learn. He stated that 10 minutes should be enough time for anyone to go to sleep, and so I instructed him in the following way: Put the book with those irregular French verbs that you hate learning so much on your bedside table, and notice that it is there before you turn your light off. If you are not asleep in 10 minutes, get out of bed, take that book down to the kitchen, and study those verbs for exactly one hour. Don't reward yourself with coffee. Go back to bed, and if you are not asleep in another 10 minutes, you can have the benefit of another one hour exactly of studying those irregular verbs.

He learned the verbs, but not at night. He said the thought of studying them at that time of the night seemed to just put him to sleep. He uses this suggestion occasionally even now—nearly 30 years later.

"I Would Rather Not Wake during the Night"

A man in his mid-60s was waking regularly at 2:30 A.M. He would reluctantly get out of bed, make a nice hot cup of tea, listen to an hour of relaxing classical music, and then he'd return to bed and sleep until the morning. I suggested that he could make a cup of tea before he went to bed so that it would be nice and cold by 2:30 A.M. and, rather than wait to wake up, he could set the alarm for 2 A.M. When he got out of bed, he would have that nice cold cup of tea and an hour of jazz waiting for him. He shuddered at the idea of cold tea, and also jazz, as classical music was his thing. When I saw him a

---

EXERCISE: PHYSICAL RELAXATION

Sit in a comfortable chair, close your eyes, and let the muscles of your legs, body, arms, face, and scalp relax. Take your time, getting familiar with the experience. When you are feeling relaxed, notice something about the experience that will help you to remember it. What part of your body is most relaxed? When you are feeling tense, see what happens if you take a moment, close your eyes, and recall that experience. What did you notice? How can you use this? Which of your clients might benefit from such an experience?

EXERCISE: RELAXING IMAGERY

Close your eyes and let your mind drift to some peaceful scene of your choosing. Pay attention to the experience with all your senses: physical sensations, sight, smell, hearing, taste. Let yourself become familiar with some aspect of your experience, whatever it may be. Sometime later, again close your eyes and recall the experience. What did you notice? How can you use this? Which of your clients might benefit from such an experience?

---

month later, he hadn't set the alarm or made the tea, and he also had not wakened during the night.

Sometimes, simply planting the seed of an unpleasant activity will resolve the problem. This simple, time-effective intervention worked with this man and can work for your clients, too.

EXERCISE: AN ORDEAL

Identify something you hate that can be performed silently at night. Next time you have trouble going to sleep, set a time limit, and after that time, get out of bed and perform the ordeal you have previously set up for yourself. What did you notice? How can you use this? Which of your clients might benefit from such an experience?

Declarations as Pathways
to Solutions

Language Influences Actions

In the preceding chapters, we explored the way our use of language in therapy is central to bringing about change. We saw that asking "How's the problem?" produces a very different mood and direction for the counseling session from asking "What improvements have you noticed?" We examined the benefit of beginning a counseling session with inquiry about likes and pleasurable activities to foster a mood of normality and equality in the counseling relationship. The "miracle question" can assist getting past seemingly impossible blocks to the progress of the session, as well as setting homework tasks, such as "I want you to notice when things are going more the way you want them to" or "Could you do something different, and notice how that helps?" or "Perhaps you could tell me what it is that you want to continue unchanged when we talk next."

Emotions and the Body Influence Actions

The interplay of mood and emotions with the conversations we have, and the further interplay between these conversations and our body—position and movement—can provide further opportunities to enhance clients' options and point the way to solutions that would otherwise seem impossible. If the solution to our problem is on the ceiling and we are habitually looking at the floor, we will never see the solution; yet, as soon as we shift our body position, in this case lifting our gaze, the solution appears before us, transparent, and obvious.

In exploring the way language, emotions, and our body influence each other and in particular the actions we can or cannot take, a whole new world of observations appear, and with this, a whole new world of interventions. As my colleague Julio Olalla said, "We cannot intervene in a world we cannot see" (personal communication). It is the action component of language, emotions, and body that only recently is beginning to emerge from behind a 2,500-year screen of thinking of language as descriptive only, and, since Descartes, of separating thoughts and their correlated actions from the body. It is only in this century that philosophers, and biologist Humberto Maturana, have begun to consider that language, emotions, and body are inextricably connected and have a very relevant action component.

We also explored how language can generate future actions and experiences. Descriptions of the present and assessments of the past are critical if we are to make sense of and even survive in our rapidly changing world. Without attention to future actions, and the possibility of generating them, we would be condemned to a limited repetition of past actions based on past observations informed by past emotions and their embodiment. In this aspect of language, *declarations* reign supreme.

Declarations Create Possibilities

Declarations are literally the language of the future. They are the bridge between our past learning and the possibility of creating a new and different experience. These ways of speaking are a particular and specific form of language and serve to create a context, a space, a world of new actions and possibilities. They allow us to disclose a whole new set of options—a whole new world of possibilities.

This may sound like the language of snake oil salesmen. Our habitual human cynicism reminds us that words are cheap, and yet we have all experienced the results of declarations made in the past that still shape our future. When someone graduates from a university with a degree, the conferring of the degree is a declaration by the university. As a result of receiving that degree, the recipient can perform a whole range of actions that otherwise would not be possible. When I received my medical degree, I was instantly transported from the world and range of activities of a medical student and into the world of different responsibilities and a range of possible actions. I was able to work in a hospital, make decisions, prescribe medication, perform operations that before the moment of receiving the degree would have been illegal but after that moment are legal and possible. The legality, the possibility is a direct result of the declaration by the university.

But not just anyone can make a declaration and expect the world to listen. I saw on TV recently that a couple were very upset because the religious celebrant who performed their marriage ceremony was an intern, and because he was not authorized to make the declaration of marriage, they had to repeat the ceremony in the afternoon. Even if the afternoon ceremony was a word-for-word repetition of the morning version, one was binding, the other irrelevant.

Declarations and Authority

The issue here is one of authority. When we hear a declaration, we automatically begin to question the authority of the declarer by asking "Who are you to make such a statement?" or something similar. As a child, I used to wonder if actors getting married in films had to keep their fingers crossed behind their back so they wouldn't *really* be married. I can now see that the actor playing the part of the priest had no authority, so when he said "I now pronounce you man and wife," his declaration was just words. When John F. Kennedy declared "We will have a man on the moon by the end of the decade," his declaration provided the context for all that followed, resulting in the moon landing. Because he had the authority as president, any difficulty in rocket design, fuel criteria, or navigation became transformed as a result of the declaration. Before Kennedy's declaration, difficulties and limitations would have led to not going ahead, whereas after his declaration, the obstacles became transformed into questions about what was needed to develop the technologies, and history reminds us that this was achieved.

Declarations are traditionally thought of as the domain of leaders, visionaries, the movers and shakers of this world. Leaders are able to be leaders because they have the authority of popular agreement, as in democratic elections, or because they seize it by force, as in a military coup. But all of us have the capacity to make declarations in areas where we have authority. In a democratic society, we have authority to make our individual declaration at elections. We can all say (declare) that such and such is or is not a problem. In our everyday life, we can become enraged if some foolish driver nearly causes us to have an accident, and we can hang on to that rage or let it go: we have the authority, we have the capacity, we can do that, at least some of the time. When my son recently vented his frustration on the wall and kicked a hole in it, I couldn't change the fact that there was now a hole in the wall, but I could shout at him, thereby increasing his conflict, or I could ask him what he had learned from the experience, what he might do the next time he felt frustrated. He was shocked to see the hole and surprised that I didn't shout at him, and told me that he will try a pillow next time. I had the authority to get angry or not. He had the authority to declare that it would be a pillow next time. This may be a small event, but I anticipate that it will not be trivial for my son in his learning.

Declarations Are Not Promises

I am not sure who said that all human conflict was a result of the sloppy use of language, but I heard Humberto Maturana observe that most relationship problems derive from complaints about broken promises that were never made. If we don't distinguish declarations from promises, we are likely to find ourselves in trouble. A recurrent dilemma in relationships is the question of love. If we assume that "I love you" is a promise, then we need to make sure we honor that promise. If one partner asks the other "Do you still love me?" it is likely that the other partner will run some kind of inventory to check for any signs of "love." If any doubt is expressed, this can intensify the dilemma and an explosion can easily follow. This searching for evidence can be the problem, even though it is attempted as a way of solving the problem, because it assumes that love is some kind of experience like indigestion or a warm fuzzy feeling. This assumes that the "love" is there, and we can use language to describe its presence or absence.

Once we see that "I love you" can be a declaration, the whole scene changes. When "I love you" is seen as a way of creating a context for the relationship, then instead of looking for evidence, we can begin to decide what kind of loving actions are consistent with that declaration. The declaration sets up the possibility of the future—one of loving—instead of merely hoping that "it" is still there and fearing that if "it" isn't, we had better do a thorough job of covering up to avoid real trouble.

This translates to other areas, including "I can pass this exam," "I can learn to be more tolerant," "I will lose weight (exercise, etc.)." These declarations serve to create the context for the changes, but they are not the changes. New Year's resolutions are often declarations and are useful if we act on them. Too often, they are thought of as promises, and if they are not followed through, the inevitable issue of trust emerges. If we make a declaration and don't act on it, that simply means we haven't acted on it, not that we are bad, defective, or flaky.

Declarations Create the Context for Change

How often have we heard a client say "I could never do that" or "I'm not that sort of person" and act consistent with that declaration, without ever recognizing that the declaration has been made? These transparent declarations are so powerful in shaping our experience precisely because they are transparent. We don't see them, and we don't have any idea that they are having such a profound influence. A woman suffering from severe agoraphobia stated, "I could never cope with standing in a line," which was like glue keeping her problem in place. She was able to begin to change only after she was able to declare that she might be able to learn, even though she hadn't found a way previously. The shift in her declaration allowed for a shift in her experience. The possibility of learning to stand in a line appeared for the first time to her after she was able to declare that it was possible and break the grip that the previous declaration had held her in, all the more powerful because of its silence:

A man wanted counseling to help him cope with his frantic executive lifestyle, working six or seven days a week, on most days for 12–14 hours. He complained of stress and requested stress management. I was concerned that if his stress levels were reduced, he would work even harder and longer, a concern that was confirmed when I asked him. When I declared "I'm not willing to help you with your stress, because I'm not willing to hasten your early death," he was surprised, and then began to wonder what other options may be available. I had a letter from him several weeks later, with photos of his horses that he had previously been too busy to tend to and ride; now he was taking time to enjoy them, and himself. He wrote, "I don't need to work all the time," and I would claim that with that declaration, he was able to begin to design a life for himself that included time off, time with his horses, and more. His declaration came as a result of my declaration that I wasn't willing to help in the way he requested. I imagine his life has been significantly extended as a direct result of those declarations, demonstrating the generative aspect of language and the way it creates future possibilities.

Declarations Create Moods

Declarations are the royal road to moods, because as context creators, they create the range of possible actions that have a direct influence on our mood. When we are told "You have passed," we experience a very different mood from being told "You've failed." We will generate a very different mood when we tell someone "You have paranoid schizophrenia" rather than "You seem to have a deep issue around trusting others."

So often, people suffer and ask for help because they are feeling overwhelmed and state (declare) that they don't know where to begin. If we ask "What is the easiest and smallest beginning you can make?" the possibility of making a beginning appears, and the mood changes visibly.

Declarations Can Restore Dignity

As human beings, we live in a world of interpretations, of stories about our world and assessments about our experiences. These interpretations are variably useful, but in problem situations are consistently unhelpful. When someone makes a self-assessment such as "I can't do math" or "I can't manage my workload" or "I can't cope with my violent husband," it's easy for that person to extrapolate that assessment so it becomes "I'm an inadequate person." The individual's integrity, legitimacy, and dignity are in question. By simply suggesting that such a person could say instead "I'm not going to do math" or "I need to find a better way of managing my workload" or "I'm no longer willing to put up with violence from my husband," assessments are put aside. By reclaiming our own personal authority and making the declaration, our mood shifts from conflict and deficiency to settlement and resourcefulness.

Declarations and the Body

If someone complains of low self-esteem, no amount of re-assurance will help unless there is a coherent shift in the body. Sometimes, such a shift will follow a conversation in which the person is reminded of past achievements, other competencies, others' positive assessments; sometimes, we can foster the conversations by attending directly to the body. Someone with low self-esteem can be expected to have a stooped body, rounded shoulders, downcast eyes. Merely changing the posture can make a difference:

A woman in her early 30s asked for help with low self-esteem. She was attractive, married, employed in a position requiring decision making, but this all seemed like a sham, a pretense, as if she might be found out at any moment. She had seen other counselors and been to self-development programs, but the problem persisted.

I asked her if she would be willing to try standing differently, as an experiment. She agreed. I asked her to stand upright, with her feet slightly apart, in line with her shoulders, to lift her shoulders and raise her arms so they were just above shoulder height and open as if to welcome the space in front of her, to lift her head so that her gaze was just higher than horizontal, and to breathe comfortably.

When she settled into this position, which took a few moments, I asked her to say "Here I am!" After a few trials in which she spoke in different tones, her mood was palpably different. Her eyes shone, she smiled, and she turned to me, looked me in the eye, and said "I can do it! I can do it!" The change in her body, the change in her mood, the change in her conversation allowed her to resign from the position she had stayed in out of fear and apply for another that she wanted. I don't know if her application was successful, but her learning to increase her self-esteem was.

Other declarations I find useful in such situations include "I am a legitimate person," "I have rights," I am entitled," and "Who I am is okay." Any follow-up counseling goes predictably easier after such an experience. Because the declaration is made in a body that can "hold it," there is a good chance that the experience can result in learning taking place, and the learning can be expected to stick. This doesn't mean that there is nothing else to do, but frequently the person is changed as a result:

A man in his 20s wanted assertiveness training. He reported having difficulty saying no and was suffering as a result. I asked him to stand firmly and solidly in front of a mirror so he could see his own face in it and say aloud "I am not going to do that." Each time he made the declaration, I asked him how believable he sounded, and after some practice, he began to articulate the no in a way that was believable. The mirror served to provide feedback so he could observe his own face and make the adjustments needed to let the experience "take."

When we hear someone making a declaration, we automatically question that person's authority. When a child says "I'm going to cook dinner tonight," we don't get out the pots and pans. We automatically recognize the child's lack of authority and we don't take the comment seriously. Politicians have a reputation of making declarations and are criticized for not keeping their promises. But declarations, as we have seen, are not promises, they do not require actions; they serve to create a space, a context in which such actions can take place. Kennedy's declaration to have a man on the moon didn't put a man on the moon. The woman declaring "Here I am" didn't create any actions. Each declaration sets the possibility for those actions; by making the declaration that the actions are possible, they become so.

Declarations and Learning

When we approach a new topic, or a new method, or a new opportunity, we can begin to move immediately into exploring and learning, or we hold back, doubting our ability to learn. How many times have we made a declaration to ourselves that "This is too hard for me" or "I could never learn this"? Often, we prove ourselves correct. We have also had the experience of saying to ourselves "I can manage this," "This won't be too bad," or even "This will be easy" and proving ourselves correct yet again. One of the attitudes most useful to learning is in the declaration "I am open to learning this," so that the possibility of learning is created in our declaring and we have the opportunity of developing that learning that otherwise might have been difficult or even impossible. I recall my first interaction with a computer 10 years or so ago. I knew I would never manage it.

DECLARING

❖ What would you like to achieve that is realistic?

❖ What emotion would sustain such an outcome?

❖ What body position would contain this experience?

Place your body in the chosen position, generate or recall the chosen emotion, look out into the distance or in a full-length mirror, and say:

❖ "I am going to achieve (the declared goal)."

❖ Notice the body and ask "How does my body feel?"

❖ Notice the emotion and ask "How was that emotion?"

❖ Ask "Did I believe what I was saying?" or "If I were listening to that, would it be believable?"

Correct any discrepancies and repeat.

Practice until the emotion and the body are coherent and solid.

Learning how to work with the enemy became possible only after I declared (decided) to give it a try. The rest is history, and the enemy is now a valued helper.

We need to be very clear that in creating possibilities by declarations we are producing just that—possibilities. But isn't that one of the main points of counseling, or living our life to the fullest: to increase possibilities?

Conclusion

Because each client is a unique individual, we are going to be most useful if we develop our observational skills so we can best see who our client is and who the client is becoming. The more observational skills we have, the more options we can generate with our clients to assist them in creating and living their own solutions.

If all we use to observe is language, we will spend most of our time exploring cause and effect and looking for explanations, as if that will provide answers. If we explore the action aspect of language, we have another point of observation and movement. If we add in observation of emotions and the body, already there is a much richer texture in the therapeutic interaction. If we further begin to observe the opportunities to intervene at the level of emotions and the body, the range of possible futures expands dramatically. These additional sets of distinctions and awareness that we can now bring to the counseling session can assist our clients in generating a future that is satisfying and autonomous, and at the same time contribute to our personal and professional satisfaction.

CHAPTER SEVEN

Ethics: An Evolution

ETHICS ARE A CENTRAL CONCERN in any human endeavor, but perhaps particularly those dealing with people's concerns, their problems, their lives. Yet ethics and ethical concerns are not isolated phenomena. They change in a flow that is timely and coherent with the general social drift. As society changes, individuals in that society will be influenced and have changing concerns. Our counseling approach needs to change to match those changing concerns. This brings the issue of ethics to the fore, perhaps as never before. In a solution-oriented approach, are we limiting our clients' experience of the fullness of their suffering; in a problem-solving approach, are we subjecting our clients to a return to a previous trauma and so risking retraumatizing them?

Minimal Standards to Belong to a Club

In the Oxford dictionary, the first definition of ethics refers to the minimal standards, the minimal requirements to belong to a club. Ethics committees deal with people doing something unethical; in the maintenance of minimal standards, they are not concerned so much about ethics as the lack of ethics. If someone does not abide by the rules, that person is thrown out of the club. If someone doesn't meet the minimal standards, that person is expelled from that community.

The fundamental notion in this definition of ethics is concerned with belonging. If you want to be a member of the American Psychological Association, for example, there are certain things that you have to do. If doctors do something they shouldn't do, they can expect an ethical inquiry. Ten years ago, the medical board sent me a letter when someone wrote an article in the newspaper about my work; the board was very sensitive about advertising at that time and wanted to know if I had approached the journalist or if the journalist had approached me. If I had approached the journalist, it would have been advertising, and I could have been fined or rebuked—it would have been unethical.

Toward Excellence

Another definition of ethics in the Oxford dictionary refers not to minimal standards but to human duty in its widest extent. Thus, an ethical approach to working in clinical circumstances demands that we contribute maximally to clients' health, that we do what is in their best interest. This shifts the focus from minimal standards to a concern for excellence: it's not about doing the least to stay safe, but rather how to be most useful.

Increasing Options

When Heinz von Foester stated that the ethical imperative is to increase options, he was talking not only about therapy but about life in general. We have often said in our work that because problems have fewer options and solutions are characterized by a range of options, it makes sense clinically to increase options. But von Foester insists that this is an ethical issue. I agree that we have an ethical responsibility, even, as von Foester says, an imperative, to increase options for our clients. I believe also that this responsibility, even imperative, extends to education, of students and of our family members, so they can have the opportunity to realize their full potential.

Learning to Live Together

Humberto Maturana claims that learning to live together is the prime human ethic. I think it is the most pressing contemporary issue that our ethics needs to address. Our world, the world of the Internet, cyberspace, and international travel, is changing at an escalating rate. One Thursday I was in Melbourne and the next Thursday I was back after traveling to another country where people had come from Venezuela, Chile, and Mexico as well as the United States and Australia. These people with different languages, different backgrounds, different cultures, and different histories, all worked together, an experience that is becoming increasingly common. It was superb.

When we don't learn to work together, to live peacefully together, we have conflict. When one group of people claim "Our way is the right way and your way is the wrong way" and another group says "No, our way is the right way and your way is the wrong way," there is conflict and enmity.

Our world is a shrinking, mobile, multicultural community with increasing complexity. We can't avoid it. We can no longer say that my way is right and your way is wrong. In our clinical work, the mood and the concerns that we are attending to invite us to give less attention to what is the right way to do things, what is the right way for clients to respond, and more attention to what we and they can do to solve their problems. We want to increase their options, but underpinning all of that is the concern How can we work effectively with this client?

I think that living together is an issue that we need to put in an ethical domain, as an ethical concern with practical repercussions. When I see this ethical shift away from rules and toward living together, I see it paralleling a social change. Previous eras were concerned with the minimal rules required to remain in a club, with worries about control, maintaining power in a hierarchy, and giving authority to someone who could say "You're in" or "You're out." These days, we don't have the choice of in or out: we're all in this soup together.

One of the challenges of the solution-oriented approach is to maintain a balance as we attempt to increase options for our clients, to assist them to live in the world we share, and at the same time, to be socially responsible. There are some options we want to decrease—violence, sexual abuse—and there are some aspects of living together that should be changed rather than tolerated—racial and gender discrimination, continuing poverty and starvation. This balance is a highly personal experience. The solution-oriented approach is not for all therapists. Some simply do not like it, and why should they? It is one way—in my experience, a useful, respectful, effective way—but still only one way, and I find it important to remind myself that problem-focused, pathology-oriented approaches also have their place.

One of my joys in teaching solution-oriented therapy is seeing how a group of disparate individuals at the beginning of a program come together by the end of it, living together, sharing, learning things we didn't know before. For me, this is ethics at its best.

> Every human act takes place in language. Every act in language brings forth a world created with others in the act of coexistence which gives rise to what is human. Thus every human act has an ethical meaning because it is an act of constitution of the human world. The linkage of human to human is, in the final analysis, the groundwork of all ethics as a reflection on the legitimacy of the presence of others. (Maturana & Varela, 1988, p. 247)

REFERENCES

Anderson, W.T. (1990). *Reality is not what it used to be.* San Francisco: Harper & Row.

De Shazer, S. (1988). *Clues: Investigating solutions in brief therapy.* New York: Norton.

Echeverria, R. (1994). *Ontologia del Lenguaje.* Santiago, Chile: Dolmen Estudio.

Erickson, M.H. (1981). [Audiotape]. *Hypnosis in psychiatry: The Ocean Monarch Lecture.* New York: Irvington.

Erickson, M.H. (1989). In E. Rossi & L. Ernest (Eds.), *The collected papers of Milton H. Erickson on hypnosis.* New York: Irvington.

Facey, A.B. (1981). *A fortunate life.* Melbourne, Australia: Penguin.

Foester, Heinz von. (1984). On constructing a reality. In P. Watzlawick (Ed.), *The invented reality: How do we know what we believe we know?* (p. 61). New York: Norton.

Frankl, V.E. (1959). *Man's search for meaning, and introduction to logotherapy.* London: Hodder and Stoughton.

Garfield, S., & Bergin, A.E. (1994). *Handbook of psychotherapy and behavior change.* New York: Wiley.

Lustig, H. (1975). [Videotape]. *The artistry of Milton H. Erickson, M.D.* Haverford, PA: Lustig.

Madanes, C. (1999, July/August). Rebels with a cause. *Family Therapy Networker,* 44.

Maturana, H.R., & Varela, F.J. (1988). *The tree of knowledge–the biological roots of human understanding* (p. 246). Boston: Shambala.

O'Hanlon, B., & Bertolino, B. (1998). *Even from a broken web: Brief, respectful solution-oriented therapy for sexual abuse and trauma.* New York: Wiley.

O'Hanlon, W.H., & Weiner-David, M. (1989). *In search of solutions: A new direction in psychotherapy.* New York: Norton.

Pisar, S. (1979). *Of blood and hope.* London: Cassell.

Watzlawick, P., Weakland, J., & Fisch, R. (1974). *Change: Principles of problem formation and problem resolution.* New York: Norton.

INDEX

185